Best Flies for Idaho

GREYCLIFF BEST FLIES SERIES
VOLUME 1

Best Flies for Idaho

by Greg Thomas

GREYCLIFF PUBLISHING COMPANY

HELENA, MONTANA

Fly photographs by Doug O'looney

Designed and typeset in Minion and Minion Display, by Geoffrey Wyatt

Cover design by Geoffrey Wyatt

Printed by Advanced Litho Printing, Great Falls, Montana

10 09 08 07 06 05 04 03 02 01 00   10 9 8 7 6 5 4 3 2 1

Best Flies for Idaho
1-10-2000
CIP for copyright page

Library of Congress Cataloging-in-Publication Data

Thomas, Greg.
    Best flies for Idaho/by Greg Thomas.
        p.cm. — (Greycliff best flies series ; vol. 1)
    Includes bibliographical references (p.).
    ISBN 1-890373-02-8 (alk. paper)
    1. Flies, Artificial—Idaho. 2. Fly fishing—Idaho. I Title. II. Series.

SH451.T46 2000
688.7'9124'09796—dc21   99-089454

CONTENTS

Acknowledgments

WITHOUT THE HELP OF MANY PEOPLE this book simply would not have been possible—don't confuse that statement with the standard carrot that authors hand out to their broad sources.

Instead, I offer that thanks because I could not have assembled such a complete project without several people's knowledge and contribution, which included personally tied flies, tying instructions, advice on fishing specific patterns on specific waters, and directions to reach other Idaho tyers who deserved inclusion in this book.

I am a sincere fly fisher and a self-taught, adequately functional fly tyer who spends a couple hundred days a year on western waters. However, I usually fish by myself and I do not belong to any organizations, so I haven't met many of my brethren. And I am too young to have met any of Idaho's historic tyers.

Therefore, I needed to speak with anglers and fly tyers who have enjoyed most of their lives in Idaho—and two of the best sources are Bruce Staples, who lives in Idaho Falls, and Marv Taylor, who lives in Boise.

Staples is a fly-fishing and fly-tying addict who is also an excellent historian. Staples learned the fly-tying trade from such legendary tyers as Bing Lempke and Stan Yamamura and he has personally met most of Idaho's top fly tyers.

Staples is also an author and one of his best productions is *Snake River Country,* a book that covers eastern Idaho's diverse trout fishing options. The book also covers the best flies to fish in that region, many of which I've included in *Best Flies for Idaho.*

For *Best Flies,* Staples is credited with tying the Bucktail Caddis, Beadhead Peacock Leech, Dry Muddler, Light Variant, Stan's Hopper, LC Moose, Marcella's Trout Fly, Sofa Pillow, Trude, Super Renegade, Loop-Wing Dun, Teton King and Queen, Marabou Jughead, Moss Caddis Emerger, North Fork Fly, and Stan's Willow Fly. For his contributions and advice, and for putting up with my numerous phone calls, I can't thank Bruce enough.

Joe Ayre of Pocatello is a good friend of Staples and he is one of eastern Idaho's best fly tyers. I thank Joe for contributing Lempke's Extended-Body Green Drake and Bing's Hopper—they are beautiful renditions of historic patterns, obviously tied by a connoisseur of precisely tied flies.

To cover the west side of the state, I relied heavily on the knowledge of Marv Taylor, a fly-fishing and fly-tying fanatic who contributed an outdoor column to the *Boise Statesman* for twenty years. During that time and through his column, Taylor divulged the merit of Idaho's prime patterns while developing his own arsenal of killer flies.

Taylor is a still-water trout fishing fanatic who wrote *Float-Tubing the West*. In that book, Taylor covers all of his vice-creations; in *Best Flies* for Idaho I've included some of Marv's most productive patterns, the flies that Marv believes no Idaho fly fisher should do without. For *Best Flies,* Marv contributed Marv's Halloween Fly, the Blond Stayner, the Little Jewell, Marv's Fly, the Taylor Shrimp and the Horsethief Leech, all developed from his own vice. He also tied the Trueblood Otter Nymph, Trueblood's Integration, and the Stayner Duck Tail, two classic patterns that arose from the vices of prominent Idaho fly fishers.

I must also thank Clayne Baker of Boise, a fly-fishing and fly-tying devotee who ran Stonefly Anglers for many years. Baker provided lots of historical information on fly patterns and he tied the Sadie Thompson Woolly Bugger, a great stillwater pattern, that is described in this book.

Warren Schoth, who runs Riverborn Fly Company in Wendell, Idaho, also contributed information to *Best Flies* and he provided several excellent patterns, including the Master Nymph, Neon Prince Nymph, Hare's Ear Rubber Leg

Nymph, Magic Perch, Malad Ant, N.A. Steelhead Bugger (aka Volcano Bugger), and the Idanha Yellow Jacket.

Greg Webster, who runs a nice fly shop in Mackay Idaho, near the banks of the Big Lost River, just downstream from Mackay Reservoir, provided the Mackay Special for inclusion in *Best Flies*.

Dan Curtis who grew up in Rathdrum, Idaho, but now works for Frontier Anglers in Dillon, Montana, contributed lots of historical information and he tied these patterns for inclusion in *Best Flies*: the Elk Hair October Caddis, October Caddis Larva, Moose Mane Extended-Body Green Drake, Sculpin Minnow, and the TLF Midge.

Scott Schnebly, who runs Lost River Outfitters in Ketchum, Idaho, and guides extensively on the Salmon River for steelhead and Silver Creek for giant rainbows and browns, provided several of his most successful patterns. For steelhead he tied the Black Bunny Leech and, after a little prodding (begging?), he offered the Fifi. He also tied the Philo Betto, which catches salmonids wherever decent sculpin populations are found.

I must also thank these eastern-Idaho fly-tying legends—René and Bonnie Harrop and Mike Lawson. You will find many of their tremendous patterns, which were developed for the Henry's Fork River, in *Best Flies*.

René Harrop provided these patterns: the Slow Water Caddis, CDC Transitional Dun, CDC Rusty Spinner, and the Short Wing Emerger. Lawson offered the Henry's Fork Hopper, Lawson's Hen Spinner, Lawson's Floating Nymph, Lawson's Brown Drake Nymph, Lawson's Green Drake Paradrake, his Henry's Fork Yellow Sally, and Lawson's Foam Beetle.

Thanks to Paul Stimpson for sending the Box Canyon Stone that he tied for Mims Barker's shop in Odgen, Utah, and to Matt King and Chris Strainer of Cross Currents in Helena, Montana, for filling the final gaps with the Blue

Winged Olive, Cased Caddis, Dahlberg Diver, Northern Pike Fly, and Swannundaze Chironomid.

Thanks also to Umpqua Feather Merchants for providing the Boss, Clouser's Crayfish, Extended-Body Olive Dun, Hemingway Caddis, Mickey Finn, Whitlock's Mouserat, and Mike Lawson's Hen Spinner, Henry's Fork Yellow Sally, and Floating Nymph.

I offer sincere thanks to the aforementioned contributors and to those folks that I spoke with briefly while tracking down Idaho's top fly tyers. I also want to thank my roommates, Mike Bordenkircher, John Huber, and Mike Whitthar, who extricated a size-2 streamer hook from the bottom of my toe—that barbed hook fully imbedded itself while I was tying patterns (don't tie barefoot!) for this project.

A final thanks goes out to those shops and individuals who took time to fill out the *Best Flies* survey. Their contribution offered a broad selection of prime flies that Idaho's top guides carry with them.

Introduction

Nowhere in the West, possibly nowhere in the world, are so many prime dry-fly streams located in such a confined area as those harbored within the borders of Idaho.

Take a look. Idaho offers the well-known and heavily-fished Henry's Fork River and Silver Creek, but it also extends invitations to cast surface flies on the Big Wood, Kelly Creek, the St. Joe, the Middle Fork Salmon, the South Fork Boise, and the Selway, among many others. Those streams offer prime hatches, great dry-fly fishing, and a measure of solitude.

With so many great options out Idahoans' backdoors, it stands to reason that Idaho should harbor a strong fly-tying community—and it does just that.

Because Idaho remains a rural area, with several noted exceptions, its anglers rely on their own talents when assembling fly patterns to take astream. For instance, in many places anglers cannot just walk over to the local fly shop and buy a few *Baetis* spinners, salmonflies, or *Callibaetis* cripples when those bugs are on the water. Instead, when they find those insects on their favorite stream, they must sit down at the fly-tying vice and create the proper imitation. This saves them long drives to the nearest cities and allows them to spend more time on the water, not on the road.

That self-reliant tradition began in the early 1900s and it continues today. For these reasons, Idaho has produced and still contains some of the most noted, innovative, and talented fly tyers in the nation.

Contained in the following pages, you'll find many fly patterns that originated in Idaho and work especially well on the Gem State's waters. With each pattern, you'll learn the lore behind the fly—who invented it, where it was first fished, and why it is so effective. Plus, you'll learn what materials are needed to reproduce the fly.

More than anything else, *Best Flies for Idaho* should

improve your fishing. These patterns are proven on Idaho's best trout streams and you can't argue with success.

I've fished most of Idaho's top trout waters extensively and I've probed many lesser-known streams during three- or four-day excursions. During those trips, I've packed many of these "Idaho" patterns with me and I rarely walk away from a stream disappointed or lacking a decent imitation of a specific insect. There is no substitute for the right fly pattern, especially when you encounter skeptical trout.

Read through the pages of this book, give thanks to the people who created these patterns, then nestle in behind your vice and go to work. Take these patterns to your favorite waters and give them a try. You won' be disappointed. Good luck on the stream.

Best Flies for Idaho

CHAPTER ONE
Fly Tyers of Idaho

HISTORIC FLY TYERS

IDAHO BOASTS AN EXTENSIVE, interesting fly-tying history, with many innovative patterns and intriguing characters.

If you were required to choose the most innovative of Idaho's thousands of patterns (no easy proposition), you might do well to choose the Trude.

The Trude was created by Carter Harrison in 1901 while visiting the Trude family's Algenia Ranch. Harrison presented the fly to A. S. Trude as a joke. However, that "joke" caught fish and its wing set off a fly-tying revolution.

Tied to imitate large stoneflies, especially *Pteronarcys californica* and *Hesperoperla pacifica*, the Trude brought large fish to the surface early after its inception. Its wing, which is tied aft of the hackle in a downwing, "fluttering" fashion, offers a perfect stonefly imitation. It's also an accurate rendition of many caddis species.

Harrison's original Trude spawned numerous progeny, including the super-effective Royal Trude. Today, the Trude's wing style is present on many of the West's most prominent patterns.

Idaho has produced many fine fly tyers, and their creations have provided many hours of joy for Rocky Mountain fly fishers. Some of Idaho's finest tyers set up camp in eastern Idaho in the early to mid-twentieth century. And who could blame them? Eastern Idaho offers a variety of waters, including spring creeks, freestone streams, tailwater rivers, and still waters, where all types of flies could be adequately tested over a variety of trout species.

One of eastern Idaho's most prolific and popular tyers was

*Bing Lempke
(Photograph by
Brad Stoddard,
courtesy Bruce
Staples)*

Bing Lempke, who created such godsends as his Extended-Body Dun, Bing's Hopper, and Lempke's Salmon Fly. Although Lempke is best known for his fly patterns, he is equally remembered as a kind, generous man who passed his expertise to hundreds of young tyers through classes and seminars, often inviting people to his home for personal lessons. That is a trait that runs consistently through Idaho's fly-tying community, and it persists today (for some reason, Idaho's fly tyers are some of the most down-to-earth, generous folks I've ever met.) Unfortunately, Lempke passed away in 1991.

Stan Yamamura is another eastern-Idaho fly-tying legend, and in the spirit of Lempke, Yamamura also handed down his skills to a younger generation through

*Stan Yamamura,
in striped shirt
(Photograph by
James McCue,
courtesy Bruce
Staples)*

classes and seminars. Yamamura spent most of his time fishing the rivers of eastern Idaho, such as the Henry's Fork, the South Fork Snake, and the Teton. He is best known for creating the North Fork Fly, Stan's Hopper, and Stan's Willow Fly.

Although Yamamura and Lempke are remembered for a number of patterns, Ardell Jeppsen's name is inscribed in the history books for one particular pattern: the Super Renegade. Jeppsen created the Super Renegade from his hospital bed while fighting polio. To fish eastern Idaho's South Fork Snake River without having a couple of these flies with you is, well, crazy. The Super Renegade, with its multicolored chenille body and fore and aft–style hackles, is a cutthroat killer.

Idaho's fly-tying history isn't limited to the eastern part of the state. Other sections of Idaho have produced killer patterns, and among the best of those is Ruel Stayner's Ducktail.

Stayner, who lived in Twin Falls, first introduced the fly through Marv Taylor's outdoor column in the *Boise*

Statesman. According to Taylor, the fly was mis-named and, unfortunately, the name stuck.

"I asked Ruel what we should call the fly and he wrote down on a piece of paper, 'the Ducktail.' I wrote the column and called the fly a Ducktail and Ruel called me back and said, 'It's supposed to be the Duckwing.' He'd written it down wrong on the piece of paper and that is why the fly is called a Ducktail even though the mallard feather is tied as the wing. Today, if I was forced to choose one fly to fish on lake or stream for the rest of my life, I would pick the Stayner Ducktail. Big fish eat little fish wherever you go, and the Ducktail is an excellent small-fish imitation."

Ruel Stayner at Sheep Creek Reservoir in the mid-1970s (Photograph by Marv Taylor)

Possibly Idaho's best-known outdoor writer, Ted Trueblood tromped around the hills and streams of Idaho when they were pure and uncrowded. Not regarded as particularly tech-nical, Trueblood's patterns are honored today, not for beauty, but for catching fish, (which, in my mind, is as it should be).

Marv Taylor had the opportunity, on sever-al occasions, to spend time with Trueblood at Trueblood's home in Nampa, and he recalled the writer as a gentle, generous man.

Ted Trueblood (Courtesy Idaho Department of Fish and Game)

"I watched him tie lots of flies, but the Otter Nymph was his greatest contribution to fly tying and fly fish-ing," Taylor said. "That pattern still works well today. Ted was a giant of the outdoor literary world, but he maintained a gentle disposition and was well-respected by all fly fisher-men."

Marv Taylor also knew George Biggs of Jerome, who cre-ated another of Idaho's most effective patterns, the inspira-tion for which came to him when another of his flies began to unravel.

"One day Biggs was fishing a reservoir and the grizzly hackle came untied on his fly," Taylor said. "It draped over the back of the fly and he really started catching fish. Biggs was always an advocate of Fore and Aft flies, so he went home and tied several flies with an aft hackle and a grizzly hackle draped over the back. But that didn't quite satisfy him, so he put mallard flank fibers on it and found it worked excellent. The fly became known as the Sheep Creek Special even though everyone around Twin Falls called it the Biggs Fly."

Armed with only the patterns developed by Trueblood, Jeppsen, Lempke, Stayner, Biggs, and Yamamura, an Idaho fly fisher could ply every water in the state and select a fly to match any hatch. However, there are hundreds, if not thousands, of historic patterns that work well on Idaho's waters. Some of these patterns continue to gain prominence, while others rest in the obscurity of individual fly boxes. Certainly, there are many other fly tyers, known only to their close companions, who deserve mention in this book. The tyers listed above are simply some of the most noted personalities in Idaho, and the flies listed are some of the most noted patterns that have originated in Idaho.

One thing that holds true with all of the historic patterns is this: They still work.

In fact, last spring I carried a couple Lempke Salmon Flies to the South Fork Boise River and proceeded to catch and release a dozen solid rainbows on the pattern. Lempke's Salmon Fly, even when battered and falling apart at the seams, worked as well as the standard, modern patterns that my buddies used.

In the evening on the same day, the stonefly action lessened, but the caddis hatch came off strong and the fish took notice. I watched my friends tie on the modern and highly effective X-Caddis and CDC Spent Caddis patterns, but they took no more fish than I did—to the end of my line I'd tied a caddis classic called the Elk Hair Caddis.

At the end of the day, just after dark, we pulled the drift boat on to its trailer and headed up a long, narrow dirt grade that leads out of the South Fork Canyon. As we dodged potholes, I marveled at the ingenuity of our fly-tying predecessors. As you will find out, the classic patterns aren't as outdated as some might think. Give them a try.

MODERN FLY TYERS

TWO OF IDAHO'S BEST-KNOWN and most innovative fly tyers herald from eastern Idaho's Henry's Fork area, and there is good reason for that: The Henry's Fork River, with its plethora of insect hatches, offers fly tyers the opportunity to test new patterns on all types of water.

Because the Henry's Fork has a spring-creek section (called the Railroad Ranch) it has become a source for some of the most technical fly patterns ever devised. And most of those patterns can be traced back to René and Bonnie Harrop, who run the House of Harrop in St. Anthony, and to Mike Lawson, who runs the Henry's Fork Anglers at Island Park.

Harrop began tying flies early. As he said, "I was born into it." He was an avid teenage fly fisher, but he couldn't afford to buy the number of flies that his passion demanded. To compensate, he chased farm animals through the barnyard, getting fur and feathers whenever possible. From those materials—"Some of the hackles were actually quite good," Harrop recalled—he created tiny mayfly patterns that worked on the Henry's Fork and launched his career.

René Harrop (Photograph by Bonnie Harrop, courtesy House of Harrop)

"The Henry's Fork is a demanding river, so I got

the idea of [creating] perfect imitations of stream insects," Harrop said. "By the time I'd spent a dozen years tying for myself, I'd become fairly accomplished. At that time, interest in the region was really increasing, so in 1967 I started tying part-time and selling to local sporting goods stores. Anyone that was en route to, or from, West Yellowstone got some of my patterns. A year later the demand for my flies was great enough that my wife, Bonnie, and I quit our jobs, and we've never looked back."

Although they may not have looked back, they may have looked at each other with saucer-like eyes when their first professional order arrived: a request from Colorado for 500 dozen dry flies, all size-20 or smaller!

"There were never enough tiny dry flies available at that time, so that's where we established our niche," Harrop said. "We saw that as a really open area in the industry—a need for delicate mayfly imitations."

Despite his antics as a child, chasing roosters around the barnyard, much of Harrop's success stems from his use of

*Mike Lawson
(Photograph by
Barry and Cathy
Beck)*

prime materials. Mike Lawson is also a proponent of fine materials, and he, too, secures his in a unique fashion.

Many of Lawson's innovative patterns require materials that are indigenous to eastern Idaho. By working with local people, Lawson is not required to part with his entire wallet to obtain quality.

"René and I, we're from the old school," Lawson said. "We're from that school of fly tyers who are also scroungers. We find materials at a decent price that we have prime access to."

For instance, Lawson said the CDC feathers on the ducks and geese he shoots during fall are of a much higher quality than what you may find at a fly shop. And, because Lawson has access to premiere Hungarian partridge capes (from local hunters and from the birds that he and his sons shoot), he incorporates high-quality partridge into many of his patterns.

"That stuff is hard to get on the commercial level," he said. "When I started tying flies for shops, I got good-quality capes from hunters. That's something the competition couldn't really compete with. We just utilized those materials that we had easy access to and other people did not.

"I'd go to fly shop owners and tell them what I had. I told them which of the flies would be superior to the ones they had. They could see a difference in the quality and they started buying my flies."

While Lawson and Harrop are well-known for their incredibly effective spring-creek patterns, Marv Taylor is recognized for his excellent still-water patterns, which are not nearly as delicate but are equally effective.

Taylor is especially well-known in the Boise area, where his outdoor column ran for twenty years. Often, Taylor included a "Fly of the Week," which introduced such excellent patterns as the Sheep Creek Special (also known as the Biggs Fly) and Ruel Stayner's Ducktail. Over the years, Taylor's column became a historical register for Idaho's outdoor events and innovative fly patterns.

Marv Taylor with bluegill at Crane Falls Lake (Photograph by Peter Barrett, courtesy Marv Taylor)

Today, Taylor continues to tie effective patterns, and he fishes as often as he can. His column ended with the Boise paper, but he now writes for the *Idaho Falls Post Register* from April through October.

Several of Taylor's patterns gained prominence in the Boise area, including a streamer called the Marv's Fly and a shrimp and snail imitation called the Taylor Shrimp. The Marv's Fly is becoming a standby for Idaho's still-water fly fishers—especially when matching damselflies. And the Taylor Shrimp is a pattern that its creator says he wouldn't be without when approaching a lake, reservoir, or tailwater stream.

Taylor, who was born and raised in Nampa, Idaho, and now lives in Boise, has also produced patterns that are variations of several classics. For example, Taylor's Blond Stayner closely resembles Ruel Stayner's tremendously effective Ducktail. However, Taylor's pattern has a golden hue, which makes it more effective than the original pattern when fishing for trout in waters infested with yellow perch.

Clayne Baker also resides in Boise, after having recently retired from his job at Stonefly Anglers. Baker possesses a wealth of fly-tying information, and several of his patterns have gained acclaim, especially in southern Idaho. Baker teaches many fly-tying classes, and he heads the Woolly Buggers Kids' Club, which teaches tying and fly fishing to Boise's youth.

One of Baker's most popular patterns is the Sadie Thompson Woolly Bugger, a red streamer that is especially effective in the desert reservoirs, such as Magic, Mormon, and Sheep Creek. Stonefly Anglers sells hundreds of dozens of this pattern each year, a testament to its effectiveness and to Baker's skill at the vice.

Bruce Staples (Photograph by Carol Staples, courtesy Bruce Staples)

Bruce Staples is a successful writer who resides in Idaho Falls. His knowledge of historic and modern fly tyers makes him one of the finest sources on the subject in Idaho. He is active in the fly-fishing community and has been teaching fly-tying classes for twenty years. Perhaps no man is more knowledgeable about Yellowstone National Park's waters: Staples has fished all the major lakes and rivers as well as most of the tributaries. He has an affinity for backcountry streams, and he fishes Yellowstone's remote waters many days each year.

Several of Staples' patterns have gained prominence in eastern Idaho. The Marabou Jughead, which resembles the Muddler Minnow, is an excellent fly that incorporates a split shot with a bullet-style head. The result is a streamer that sinks quickly and requires no lead on the leader to reach the bottom, where those big eastern Idaho brown trout prefer to hide. Staples' other well-known patterns include the Beadhead Peacock Leech, the Dry Muddler, and the Loop-Wing Dun. Staples has authored several books, including *River Journal: Yellowstone Park* and *Snake River Country*, which contain excellent information on eastern Idaho's and Yellowstone Park's tremendous fisheries.

As with the historical section, this list of modern tyers is but a sampling of Idaho's best fly tyers.

CHAPTER TWO
FLY PATTERNS
An Alphabetical List of Recipes

With black-and-white and color
photographs by Doug O'looney

Adams (mayfly/caddisfly)

Hook: TMC 900BL, sizes 10–20	
Thread: Gray	
Wing: Grizzly hen hackle fibers, tied upright and divided	
Tail: Moose hair	
Body: Gray dubbing or muskrat	
Hackle: Grizzly and brown	
Butt (optional): Yellow Antron to imitate egg-laying female	

THE ADAMS MAY BE THE MOST POPULAR dry fly ever. Since its inception in Michigan in the early 1920s, it has been cast in every trout-laden country and water type in the world.

Created by Len Halladay, the Adams' success can be attributed to its versatility: Depending on what color dubbing is used and what size it is tied, the Adams represents every imaginable mayfly dun, and it doubles as a decent midge or mosquito imitation. Dubbed with a pale yellow body in sizes 14 to 18, the Adams is an excellent Pale Morning Dun imitation. When you tie the Adams with the traditional gray body in sizes 14 to 18, few trout will refuse it when *Callibaetis* mayflies emerge on flat-water spring creeks, such as the Henry's Fork Railroad Ranch section, Silver Creek's Sullivan Slough, or the Bechler River Meadows. On slow-moving waters, the traditional Adams is this author's choice over the more prominent Parachute Adams, which found acclaim in the 1980s and is a standard pattern in the West today.

Whether you're fishing the aforementioned spring creeks, sedate sections of freestone streams, high-mountain lakes, lowland reservoirs, or ponds, the standard Adams will draw trout to the top.

Air Head (attractor)

Hook: Standard dry fly, sizes 8–16

Body: Brown mink dubbing with guard hairs left in for a shaggy appearance

Wing: Brown elk hair, tied in halfway down the hook shank; with body dubbed behind and in front of the wing

Head: White closed-cell foam strips (cut six or so thin strips of foam; tie them sticking out over the eye of the hook; pull them back and tie them down in a bullet head; clip a few strips from the bottom, but leave the rest of them as a collar.

Variations: Tie in yellow (with body of yellow mink dubbing and wing of yellow elk hair) and brown (with body of yellow/olive mink dubbing and wing of brown elk hair).

GARY LAFONTAINE, THE MAD HATTER of fly innovation, named this strange looking fly for the buoyant, highly visible head provided by the white closed-cell foam. It became very popular on the South Fork Snake River with float guides. Its buoyancy and ready visibility makes it an incredibly effective attractor pattern, perfect for the angler casting from a moving drift boat. The yellow version is a great match for the Yellow Sally and the brown steps in for the Early Brown Stone.

Beadhead Peacock Leech (damselfly)

Hook: Mustad 9672 3X long, sizes 4–10

Head: Brass bead

Thread: Black

Body: Peacock

Tail: Rust marabou

Rib: Gold wire

Hackle: Ginger

THE PREDECESSOR TO THIS BEADHEAD pattern dates back to the mid-1980s, but the beadhead version was first introduced by Bruce Staples in 1991. The beadhead was added to increase the fly's weight and to add attraction. When tying the fly, Staples ties the bead on loose so it makes a low frequency noise that attracts trout.

"I fish the Beadhead Peacock Leech in lakes where it simulates a damsel nymph when tied in a size 10," Staples said. "When tied on larger hooks it matches dragonflies. In streams it's an attractor that imitates minnows, leeches, and damsels. It's been a great pattern for me on the Little Wood River, especially in March and September."

Bing's Hopper (terrestrial)

Hook: TMC 900BL, sizes 6, 8, 10

Thread: Tan

Rib: Gold or silver Mylar

Body: Tan Antron or closed-cell synthetic

Legs: Knotted ringneck pheasant tail fibers in the back; divided elk hair or rock chuck tail fibers in the front

Wing: Wood duck or mallard overwing with red polar bear, bucktail, or hackle fibers for the underwing

Head: Spun antelope hair, clipped to shape

CREATED IN THE 1970s, Bing's Hopper initially lacked an extended body. Bing Lempke added this element around

1981, and his hopper continues to frequent fly boxes today, mostly around eastern Idaho. Due to its buoyancy and stability, this hopper is an excellent choice when fishing the North and South Forks of the Snake River, the South Fork Boise, the North Fork Clearwater, the Lochsa, and any other water where grassy banks meet riffled corners and choppy runs. This fly requires numerous materials and some time to tie. The hopper's head is made from spun antelope hair; rock chuck tail fibers are used for the legs; tan antron or closed-cell synthetic forms the body; .006 monofilament is often used as the beam to form the extended body; wood duck flank is used for the wing.

Bitch Creek Nymph

Hook: TMC 5263, sizes 2, 4, 6	
Thread: Black	
Tail: White or yellow rubber leg material	
Antennae: White or yellow rubber leg material	
Abdomen: Woven black and orange chenille	
Thorax: Black chenille	

Hackle: Brown

Optional: Lead weight wrapped the length of the hook shank

THE BITCH CREEK NYMPH has created a bone of contention between anglers who insist the pattern originated in Montana and a faction of Idaho fly fishers who believe it was created closer to home. Wherever the large stonefly pattern was developed, there's no arguing that it's one of the most effective nymphs in the Rocky Mountain region.

When I attended college in Missoula, Montana, the Bitch Creek was a standby. On Rock Creek, the Clark Fork, the Bitterroot, the Big Hole, the Madison, the Gallatin, the Yellowstone—wherever I threw that big bug—it produced fish.

Today, the Bitch Creek is extremely effective in the deeper runs and riffles of Idaho's premiere stonefly rivers, such as the

South Fork Snake, the Henry's Fork, the Teton, the Blackfoot, and the South Fork Boise. Although some commercial patterns are tied unweighted, the Bitch Creek works best when it's scooting along the bottom rocks in relatively deep runs, or during salmon fly emergences, when you should bounce it across the boulders and let it swing toward shore. For that reason, most tyers wrap the hook shank generously with lead wire.

Black Bunny Leech (steelhead fly)

Hook: Daiichi 2441, sizes 2, 4

Thread: Red

Tail: Eight strands of pearl Krystal Flash mixed with red Flashabou, all cut short to extend about ½ inch off the back of the hook

Body and Tail: Black bunny strip. The tail should just cover the flash material

Head: Bead eyes superglued to the hook and wrapped with red thread

BLACK IS A UNIVERSALLY GOOD COLOR for steelhead, and it works especially well on Idaho's upper and lower Salmon River.

"If I ever have to get a fish for a client, this is the fly I tie on," said Scott Schnebly, who runs Lost River Outfitters in Ketchum and fishes the Salmon River religiously. "It works well for spring and fall fish, and it's also effective when tied in red, pink, and purple. But you just can't beat black."

Blond Stayner (nymph/wet fly)

Hook: Mustad 9672, sizes 2, 4, 6, 8

Tail: Orange hackle fibers

Body: Gold and dark olive variegated chenille

Ribbing: Flat gold tinsel

Wing: Yellow-dyed wood duck

Beard: Orange hackle fibers

Head: Black thread

THE BLOND STAYNER IS A VARIATION of Ruel Stayner's immensely successful Ducktail. Created by Marv Taylor, this fly is intended to specifically imitate yellow perch, but it also matches any other golden-hued minnow, including several chub species found in Idaho.

"When you're fishing in an area that has perch, the Blond Stayner is more effective than the original pattern," Taylor said. "The whole illusion of the fly is more yellow and very similar to a perch."

Blue Winged Olive (aka BWO, mayfly)

Hook: TMC 100, sizes 16–22
Thread: Olive
Wing: Blue dun hen hackle tips, divided
Tail: Blue dun hackle fibers
Body: Olive dubbing
Hackle: Blue dun

BAETIS (BWO) HATCHES OCCUR on most Idaho streams and even on some still waters. Despite their diminutive size—most range from size 16 to 22 (some are called SOB BWOs and must be tied size 24 or smaller)—they are incredibly important in the trout's diet and are taken greedily on most waters twice a year.

Typically, *Baetis* are present in late winter and early spring, when they can be matched by size-16 and -18 imitations. They are also present on some waters throughout the summer, such as Silver Creek, the Henry's Fork, and the Big Wood River. Solid *Baetis* hatches return in September and continue through November. During the cold fall season, *Baetis* must be matched by size-18 to -24 imitations.

No matter when you encounter a *Baetis* hatch, patterns are most effective on blustery, drizzly days when duns spend the most time on the water. Standard *Baetis* patterns are tied just like an Adams with an olive body. Thorax patterns that incorporate a blue dun turkey flat as the wing are very effective on spring creeks and flat-water stretches of freestone streams, such as Kelly Creek and the Lochsa River.

While this basic pattern suffices, *Baetis* are more adeptly matched by modern patterns, such as *Baetis* cripples and loop-wing emergers.

Boss (steelhead fly)

Hook: TMC 7999, sizes 0, 2, 4

Thread: Black

Tail: Black bucktail or calf tail

Body: Black chenille

Rib: Silver tinsel

Hackle: Red or orange (long)

Head: Red or black thread with bead-chain eyes

DEVELOPED FOR THE STEELHEAD streams of northern California, the Boss made a pilgrimage north to Idaho and is effective on the Salmon and Clearwater rivers. The Boss is weighted by its bead-chain eyes, which makes it a good choice when fishing high choppy water or when trying to reach the bottom of medium-depth pools and riffles.

Box Canyon Stone (nymph)

Hook: Mustad 3906B, sizes 2, 4

Thread: Black

Tail: Brown or black goose biots

Body: Black yarn

Wing Case: Brown turkey quill

Thorax: Black yarn

Hackle: Furnace saddle hackle

NAMED AFTER THE FAMOUS STONEFLY stretch of the Henry's Fork River below Island Park Reservoir, this classic nymph is a killer on every stonefly water in the state.

The Box Canyon Stone, which was created by Mims Barker, who ran The Fly Line in Ogden, Utah, offers a dark black body, forked tail, plenty of bushy, "leggy" saddle hackle around the thorax, and is weighted to drift deep. That combination makes it as effective as any other stonefly nymph, including the Bitch Creek. The Box Canyon is most effective as a salmon fly imitation when tied on size-2 or -4 hooks. Tied in sizes 6 to 10 with tan, yellow, or olive dubbing, the Box Canyon is an effective match for golden stoneflies.

Braided-Butt Damsel

Hook: TMC 900BL, sizes 6, 8, 10

Thread: White

Wingcase: Poly yarn (tied in parachute style)

Abdomen: Braided leader

Thorax: Blue dubbing

Hackle: Blue dun (tied parachute style around poly yarn post)

Eyes (optional): Burned monofilament

THE BRAIDED-BUTT DAMSEL will not be the most often used damsel pattern in your fly box. However, when the situation calls for one, you need a Braided-Butt Damsel—when trout key on the adult damsel, strikes can be smashing.

Typically, lowland lake and reservoir trout concentrate on damsel nymphs, but occasionally they focus on the adults as they hover around the water, especially near cattails and exposed vegetation along the banks. If you see several rises near exposed vegetation, tie on the Braided-Butt and get ready for some fun.

Brassie (nymph)

Hook: TMC 200R, sizes 16–24

Thread: Black or rust

Body: Copper wire

Head: Peacock herl

Many of Idaho's best streams traditionally close November 30th. But some—such as the Big Wood, the Big Lost, the South Fork Boise, the lower sections of the South Fork and North Fork Snake and the lower St. Joe—remain open throughout the winter. When fishing those streams during the cold season, there may be no more effective pattern than the diminutive Brassie. No serious angler should head astream in Idaho without a supply of these nymphs in sizes 16 to 24. Easy to tie, the Brassie is an extremely effective midge imitation, and also doubles as a *Baetis* nymph. Due to its copper-wire body, the Brassie sinks quickly (for extra weight you can attach a split shot to the leader several inches above the nymph).

During the winter, the Brassie excels when drifted through slow-moving currents. Deep pools and eddies behind stream obstructions scream for Brassies. During summer and fall, the Brassie works well prior to, during, and after midge and mayfly hatches. At that time, when the water is warm and fish are most active, a Brassie drifted through the riffles produces nicely. It is also very effective when fished as a dropper below a dry fly.

Bucktail Caddis

Hook:	Mustad 96722, sizes 2–16
Body:	Orange floss or dubbing
Rib:	Furnace or brown saddle hackle
Wing:	Brown bucktail
Head:	Trimmed deer hair

The Bucktail Caddis remains a popular fly in Idaho, and is heralded for its versatility and visibility, especially in fast, choppy water. Depending on its size, the Bucktail Caddis may imitate a variety of caddis and stonefly species. Especially effective on freestone rivers, the bucktail also takes trout on tailwaters, such as the Henry's Fork, the South Fork Boise, and the South Fork Snake. To match giant *Pteronarcys* stoneflies and golden stoneflies (e.g., Salmon Fly, Willow Fly) tie the fly in sizes 2, 4, or 6. To match caddis and little golden stoneflies (Yellow Sally) try sizes 6 through 16.

Canadian Brown Mohair Leech (streamer)

Hook:	Standard streamer hook, sizes 4, 6, 8, 10
Thread:	Brown
Body:	Brown mohair
Tail:	Mohair fibers
Head:	Standard thread wrap or bead
Note:	Can be tied in various colors

ACCORDING TO MARV TAYLOR of Boise, a group of Idahoans regularly traveled to Alberta in the 1970s—the only place where you could find brown mohair yarn at the time. They brought it back to Idaho and tied leech patterns that were very effective at Henry's Lake and lesser-known waters, such as Horsethief Reservoir.

Taylor fished the pattern extensively in the early 1970s at Horsethief, which, at the time, was an excellent trout water (today it's often infested with yellow perch). One evening, Taylor was catching lots of fish on his leech, and his friend asked what he was using. He replied, "I'm using that Canadian brown mohair," and the name stuck. Today, the Canadian Brown Mohair Leech is one of the top still-water patterns in the world. You'll encounter it in every fly bin in the West, and the pattern has worked well wherever it's been fished. Every float-tube fly fisher in the West should carry a few of these gems.

Carey Special (streamer)

Hook:	Mustad 9671, sizes 6, 8, 10
Thead:	Olive
Body:	Peacock herl or olive dubbing
Rib:	Black thread
Hackle:	Pheasant rump

The Carey Special was created by Dr. Lloyd Day and Col. Carey of Quesnel, British Columbia, around 1925. Tied with a peacock herl body and long pheasant rump feathers extending beyond the bend of the hook, the fly was originally intended to mimic an emerging caddis. However, the Carey Special suggests a plethora of other food items, including damselfly and dragonfly nymphs. No matter what lake or reservoir you choose to fish in the Gem State, try a Carey Special.

Cased Caddis Larva (nymph)

Hook: TMC 200R, sizes 12–16

Thread: Black

Rib: Copper wire

Abdomen: Peacock herl and clipped furnace hackle

Thorax: Cream Antron

Head: Black Haretron (picked)

This pattern imitates the rock-hugging cased-caddis larvae that anglers find so often when inspecting the submerged rocks and logs of Idaho's streams. No matter where you plant your wading boots, you are likely to find some of these creatures and trout do pay attention to them. To best imitate the cased caddis' rock case, use the thickest furnace hackle you can located. Small chunks of white and brown or black foam may also be glued to the body to imitate rocks.

CDC Biot ComparaDun *Callibaetis* (mayfly)

Hook: TMC 100, sizes 14, 16, 18

Thread: Tan

Tail: Gray hackle fibers

Abdomen: Olive/tan goose or turkey biots

Thorax: *Callibaetis* Superfine Dubbing

Wing: Light dun CDC with natural mallard

THIS IS AN OUTSTANDING PATTERN during *Callibaetis* emergences. Early in the summer, *Callibaetis* usually run about size 14. However, by late summer through early fall, they should be dressed on size-16 and -18 hooks.

This pattern floats well, and its mallard wing imitates the speckled wing of the natural. I've fished this pattern successfully on many of Idaho's streams and lakes, especially in slow-water sections and eddies of tailwaters and spring creeks.

CDC Biot ComparaDun Trico (mayfly)

See photo of CDC Biot ComparaDun *Callibaetis*	**Hook:** TMC 100, sizes 20–26
	Thread: Black
	Tail: White tail fibers
	Abdomen: Olive goose or turkey biot
	Thorax: Black Superfine Dubbing

Wing: White CDC

THIS SHANE STALCUP PATTERN is especially effective during heavy Trico spinner falls on Idaho's spring creeks, such as the Henry's Fork and Silver Creek, and should have a place in your fly box during any mid- to late-summer spring-creek excursion

When Trico spinners hit the water they're often dense, which renders fly fishers helpless to find their pattern among so many naturals. The CDC wing of this pattern is extremely buoyant and visible—attributes when fishing size-20 to -26 flies. The olive body suggests a female Trico, which trout often key in on. Anglers who restrict themselves to purely black patterns, which are suggestive of the male Trico, will not enjoy as much success.

CDC *Callibaetis* Spinner (mayfly)

Hook: TMC 900BL, sizes 14–18

Thread: Tan

Tail: Light blue dun hackle fibers

Body: Tan turkey biot

Wing: Blue dun CDC

Overwing: Brown Z-Lon

Thorax: Tan Superfine Dubbing

Note: By varying color combinations and sizes, this pattern can imitate the spinners of any mayfly species

HERE'S A PATTERN THAT SERVES anglers well when fishing slow-water sections of spring creeks and tailwaters, as well as lakes and reservoirs.

Callibaetis mayflies emerge throughout the summer, and their hatches extend into early fall. They're especially abundant where current is minimal. Most of Idaho's lowland lakes and reservoirs have large *Callibaetis* populations, as do its spring creeks, such as the Sullivan Slough stretch on Silver Creek and the Railroad Ranch on the Henry's Fork.

This pattern represents the *Callibaetis* spinner that has fallen to the water with wings spread. When trout are selectively feeding on *Callibaetis* spinners, as they often do, this pattern is the choice.

CDC Rusty Spinner (mayfly)

Hook: TMC 100, sizes 14–24

Thread: Cream nylon or rust

Tail: Grizzly hackle fibers

Abdomen: Tan goose biot

Thorax: Light tan or rust Superfine Dubbing

Wing: Gray CDC or gray Hungarian partridge

See photo of CDC *Callibaetis* Spinner

THERE ARE FEW DRY FLIES MORE EFFECTIVE than the Rusty Spinner. Only the Parachute Adams, the Royal Wulff, and the Elk Hair Caddis account for more trout in Idaho.

The Rusty Spinner can be sabotaged by inexperienced fly tyers: An oversized body with little taper is a sure sign to a trout that the offering is a fake. In Idaho, you'll find such patterns in the fly bins of department stores or at roadside gas stations. Beware of a fat Rusty Spinner—it will fool only the most aggressive, gullible fish.

The CDC Rusty Spinner, tied by René Harrop, offers all the qualities that trout desire, and is one of the most popular and effective variations.

"The CDC Rusty Spinner has great flotation qualities, but it uses less material and duplicates a more realistic silhouette than other patterns," Harrop said. "By not overloading it with material, we accommodate a slimmer profile, and that is an important factor when tying and fishing spinners. On our patterns, we also use a goose-biot body to keep that slender aspect."

CDC Transitional Dun (PMD, mayfly)

Hook: TMC 100, sizes 16, 18	
Thread: Yellow	
Tail: Wood duck fibers	
Body: Blend of Antron and wool	
Wing: Medium dun CDC	

Thorax: Blended yellow and olive dubbing

Legs (optional): Butts of paired CDC tips, trimmed

SIMILAR TO THE WAY THEY BEHAVE during a Green Drake hatch, trout may key in on emergent PMD patterns, rather than those matching duns, when a particular river has been pounded ruthlessly.

In Idaho, many streams see Pale Morning Dun activity for several months. Early in the season, trout may crush

PMD adult imitations, but they get wise after a while.

"This pattern is attractive to trout because of its vulnerability," René Harrop said. "It imitates an insect that's struggling to emerge and that is the best time for a trout to eat a mayfly. This pattern also works the idea that over several months the trout see so many dun imitations that they shy away from them. This pattern has a lifelike configuration, and it differs from the standard patterns so it works throughout the season."

Chernobyl Hopper (terrestrial)

Hook: 3X-long dry-fly hook, sizes 2–8

Thread: Yellow

Underbody: Rainy's Float Foam, yellow

Overbody: Tan Float Foam cut slightly wider and longer than the underbody and glued to the underbody

Legs: White, tan, black, or gray rubber

Indicator: Red Float Foam

NOT ONLY DO I KEEP A FEW OF THESE UGLY creations in my terrestrial box, I must admit that I fish them, too. That's not something you might brag about when in the company of a purist. The Chernobyl Hopper isn't pretty, but it catches fish even on challenging streams such as the Henry's Fork.

Easy to tie and extremely durable, the Chernobyl Hopper definitely deserves a spot in your fly box. The pattern was developed in the mid-1990s, and I first fished it on Montana's lower Clark Fork, where picky rainbow trout often shun perfectly tied *Baetis*, Trico, and PMD imitations. However, instead of tearing your hair out on a hot afternoon, I found that you can tie on a Chernobyl Hopper and enjoy excellent bank fishing all day long from July through September.

Since that original experience on the Clark Fork, I've thrown the Chernobyl Hopper on many of Idaho's streams, including Silver Creek, and it has proved very effective.

Clouser's Crayfish

Hook: TMC 5263, sizes 0, 2, 4

Thread: Olive

Antennae: Pheasant tail

Nose: Natural hen mallard fibers

Back: Dark mottled turkey quill

Body: Pale gray yarn or dubbing

Claws: Natural hen mallard fibers

Rib: Gray thread

Legs: Ginger, grizzly or olive-grizzly hackle

THERE ARE MANY CRAYFISH PATTERNS in existence today and a variety of them work fine. However, as a whole, crayfish patterns are underfished. The most effective rendition I've found is Bob Clouser's dark brown turkey Crayfish. Clouser's Crayfish works well on rivers and lakes. When fishing that pattern, work it deep and deliver it in quick, short bursts, followed by a pause, which allows the pattern to sink. Often, a big brown trout will pick up the crayfish as it sinks.

Dahlberg Diver (bass and pike fly)

Hook: Mustad 3366, size 0 and 2

Thread: Red flat waxed nylon

Weed Guard: Monofilament

Tail: A few strands of gold Flashabou with black marabou feather

Skirt 1: Spun deer hair

Waist: Spun black deer hair (clipped)

Skirt 2: Tip ends of deer hair used for collar

Collar: Clipped dear hair

Head: Spun deer hair, clipped to bullet shape, flat on bottom

LARRY DAHLBERG CREATED the Dahlberg Diver, which ranks as one of the most effective bass flies in Idaho. Depending on what colors are used, the Diver may represent a variety of minnows. Bass pound it as a shiner or small trout and brown trout, in rivers and lakes, may crush it as a minnow. It is best fished with short quick strips.

Diving Caddis (wet fly)

Hook: TMC 9300, sizes 14, 16, 18	
Thread: Black	
Body: Green or tan Antron	
Wing: Brown partridge over Clear Antron	
Hackle: Brown	

ANOTHER GARY LAFONTAINE CREATION, the Diving Caddis is the fly to use when caddis return to the river during the last hour of light to deposit eggs.

"The diving caddis is a wet fly that I like to fish unweighted," LaFontaine said. "I cast upstream and let it dead-drift just under the surface. I use an Elk Hair Caddis or an X-Caddis as the dry-fly indicator and I'll drop the Diving Caddis about 9 inches behind the dry fly."

Dry Muddler (terrestrial)

Hook: Mustad 9672, sizes 4–6

Thread: Gray

Body: Gold floss

Rib: Gold tinsel

Tail: Turkey quill

Underwing: Light brown calf tail overlain with white calf tail

Head: Spun deer hair butts (clipped)

> See photo of the Muddler Minnow

VERSATILITY IS THIS PATTERN'S greatest attribute. The Dry Muddler can be fished under the surface, but on top it imitates golden stoneflies, grasshoppers, moths, and even the October caddis. When fishing the Dry Muddler give it some life—a twitch here, a strip there. Anglers should find this pattern effective on most Idaho streams.

Electric Caddis (nymph)

Hook: TMC 3761, sizes 18, 20

Thread: Olive

Rib: Fine copper wire

Back: Flat pearlescent tinsel

Abdomen: Olive dubbing

Head: Dark brown dubbing

THE ELECTRIC CADDIS IMITATES a free-swimming or net-building caddis larva, so it's most often tied in olive or cream. This pattern should be tied unweighted. However, you may have to weight the leader to get the fly down where you want it. Fishing the Electric Caddis as a dropper is also an option.

"I generally fish the Electric Caddis as a dropper and it works real well behind a larger beadhead Prince Nymph," its creator, Mike Lawson, said. "It fishes best in the small sizes, like 18 and 20, and I'll fish it dead-drift or swinging."

Elk Hair Caddis

Hook: TMC 900BL, sizes 14–20

Thread: Tan, olive, or black

Rib: Fine gold wire

Body: Tan, olive, or black Antron

Hackle: Palmered grizzly hackle dyed olive, black, or tan

Wing: Elk hair

Head: Clipped elk hair

ONE OF THE MOST POPULAR FLY PATTERNS in the West, the Elk Hair Caddis garners no less acclaim in Idaho. Created by Al Troth of Dillon, Montana, the Elk Hair Caddis works well on all types of waters, including freestone streams, tailwater rivers, mountain and lowland lakes, and even spring creeks. Little golden stoneflies may be matched with this pattern as well. The Elk Hair Caddis is an easy fly to tie, and it is extremely buoyant. All Idaho fly fishers should carry a few of these dandies in their fly box.

Elk Hair October Caddis

Hook: TMC 900 BL, sizes 6, 8

Rib: Fine gold wire

Body: Blend of golden rabbit, yellow seal, and golden retriever underfur

Hackle: Long brown saddle hackle

Wing: Elk body hair

THE ELK HAIR CADDIS WAS CREATED BY AL TROTH of Dillon, Montana, but this October variation was created by Dan Curtis of Rathdrum, Idaho, to match caddis that emerge on northern Idaho's wonderful cutthroat and rainbow trout streams during the fall.

According to Curtis, the best time to fish this pattern is when adult female caddis return to the river to deposit their eggs. Typically, anglers find egg-laying females most abundant in the afternoon and evening.

You can fish the Elk Hair October Caddis in riffled water, but it may be most effective when danced across slick glides and tailouts to simulate the actual insect. This fly floats high even in choppy water, so it's an excellent choice on freestone streams and tailwater fisheries. Expect violent strikes.

Emergent Sparkle Pupa (caddisfly)

Hook: TMC 100, sizes 16, 18

Thread: Tan, olive, or gray

Shuck: Tan, olive, or gray Antron yarn

Underbody: Tan, olive, or gray Antron yarn

Veil: Tan, olive, or gray Antron

Wing: Deer hair

Head: Dark brown Superfine Dubbing

THIS PATTERN, CREATED BY GARY LAFONTAINE of Deer Lodge, Montana, is a standby on Idaho's freestone streams and tailwaters. I find the Emergent Sparkle Pupa very effective on the South Fork Boise, the Big Wood River, the Little Wood River, the Henry's Fork, the South Fork Snake, Kelly Creek, the North Fork Clearwater River, Birch Creek, and the Big Lost River—really, any water that caddis inhabit.

LaFontaine created the pattern to imitate emerging caddis. "The reason it's special is because it's tied with Antron yarn, and that Antron mimics air bubbles you see on the actual insect."

LaFontaine suggests fishing this pattern with a greased wing so that it is only partially submerged, as is the natural. Fish the fly with a dead drift.

Extended-Body Olive Dun (mayfly)

See color photo	**Hook:** TMC 100, sizes 16, 18
	Thread: Black
	Body: Grayish olive Superfine
	Wing: Dun goose primary feather
	Hackle: Ginger

Tail: Three light dun tailing fibers

Rib: Yellow thread

ONE OF BING LEMPKE'S CLASSIC CREATIONS, the Extended-Body Olive Dun is a hit wherever spring and fall *Baetis* hatches occur. Fish it on Silver Creek in October, the Henry's Fork in late May and June, Kelly Creek in October, or on the Big Lost River in March; the Extended-Body will draw rises. Due to its realistic appearance, this pattern is especially effective on spring creeks and flat-water stretches of freestone and tailwater streams.

Fall Favorite (steelhead fly)

| **Hook:** TMC 7999, sizes 2, 4, 6 |
| **Body:** Flat, oval, or embossed silver tinsel |
| **Hackle:** Red |
| **Wing:** Orange bucktail or polar bear fur |

THIS STEELHEAD FLY ORIGINATED IN CALIFORNIA and was specifically tied for fall-run fish. However, it performed equally well on winter-run steelhead and became a mainstay in the fly boxes of Northwest steelhead anglers, including those who chase those big sea-run rainbows on Idaho's Clearwater, Snake, Little Salmon, and Salmon rivers. The Fall Favorite will take fish on all of Idaho's steelhead streams, but it is particularly effective on the Clearwater during fall.

Fifi (steelhead fly)

Hook: Mustad AC92553R (offset), sizes 0, 2

Thread: Burnt orange

Tail: Mix of red Krystal Flash and pearl Flashabou

Body: About ⅓ of a strand of orange egg yarn tied so that it lies perpendicular to the hook

Head: ⅛-inch chrome eyes cemented to the hook

See color photo

HERE'S A FLY THAT ORIGINATED AS MANY FLIES DO—by quick observation and rapid fieldwork at the vise. Scott Schnebly first tied this fly in 1992 after watching Bill Rousey from Ketchum take several steelhead from the upper Salmon River on a similar fly.

"Rousey flashed one to me in a parking lot in Stanley [Idaho], and called it the Butterfly," Schnebly said. "I quickly tied one up and he said 'It's close, but not the same.' I fished my fly anyway and it worked—man did it work!

"Now, the Fifi is the first fly I fish for spring steelhead," Schnebly added. "If a fish won't eat this fly it isn't going to eat anything and I just go and find another fish to work. I fish the Fifi just like a nymph, dead-drift under an indicator. It works especially well on the upper Salmon, but it will take fish on any small river in thin water where a nymph can be fished effectively. It works well during fall, too, but it's just a great spring steelhead pattern."

Schnebly said the fly got its name because it reminded

him of a poodle fresh from the groomer's. When tying the Fifi, Schnebly recommends taking the yarn and standing it upright, above the hook, when clipping it. Also, when clipping the yarn, roll it so that it ends up convex. The yarn should extend ⅜ to ½ inch out from the side of the hook.

Flashback Hare's Ear Nymph

See photo of Gold-Ribbed Hare's Ear	**Hook:** TMC 3761, sizes 14, 16, 18
	Thread: Tan
	Tail: Brown partridge
	Rib: Fine gold wire
	Abdomen: Hare's ear dubbing

Wingcase: Pearl or golden-olive Flashabou

Thorax: Hare's ear dubbing

Legs: Hare's ear dubbing picked from abdomen

VARIED ONLY SLIGHTLY FROM ITS COUSIN—the standard Gold-Ribbed Hare's Ear—the Flashback Hare's Ear is a nice choice when rivers and lakes run slightly off-color. Under those conditions, the flashy wingcase may be just enough to draw a trout's attention to the nymph. Tied in various sizes, the Flashback Hare's Ear is a suitable match for many mayfly species. It is particularly effective when tied to a size-16 hook, which matches Pale Morning Duns.

Flashback Pheasant Tail Nymph

See photo of Pheasant Tail Twist Nymph	**Hook:** TMC 3761, sizes 14, 16, 18
	Thread: Brown
	Rib: Fine copper wire
	Tail: Pheasant tail fibers
	Abdomen: Pheasant tail fibers

Wingcase: Pearl Flashabou

Head: Brown thread, copper wire, or copper bead

LIKE THE FLASHBACK HARE'S EAR, the Flashback Pheasant

Tail is an excellent choice when matching mayfly nymphs, especially when the water runs off-color as it can do during early-season *Baetis,* March Brown Drake, and Pale Morning Dun emergences. The Flashback Pheasant Tail is most effective when fished dead drift although it will take strikes as it rises toward the surface at the end of a drift.

Freight Train (steelhead fly)

Hook: TMC 7999, sizes 0, 2

Thread: Black

Wing: White calf tail and pearl Krystal Flash

Tail: Purple hackle fibers

Rib: Fine silver oval tinsel

Body: Fluorescent fire-orange fuzzy wool, fluorescent red fuzzy wool and black chenille

Hackle: Purple

THIS IS ANOTHER FINE RANDALL KAUFMANN CREATION that works well in Idaho. Kaufmann lives in Portland, Oregon, and the Freight Train grew in popularity on the banks of Kaufmann's local streams, especially on the Deschutes River. However the Freight Train is equally effective on the Salmon and Clearwater rivers. Overall, the Freight Train combines lots of good steelhead colors into one fine fly.

Goddard Caddis

Hook: TMC 900BL, sizes 14, 16, 18

Thread: Tan

Body: Tan caribou or deer hair

Antennae: Stripped hackle stem

Hackle: Brown or ginger

THIS PATTERN, ORIGINATED in Great Britain by John Goddard and originally used on the lakes of the United Kingdom, is a savior to nearsighted fly fishers. Spun from light-colored deer hair, this fly is extremely high-riding and graciously visible, even when fished through fast riffles. Best used to match caddisflies, the Goddard Caddis also imitates little golden stoneflies.

Gold-Ribbed Hare's Ear (nymph)

Hook: TMC 3761, sizes 14, 16, 18, 20
Thread: Black
Rib: Fine gold tinsel
Abdomen: Hare's ear dubbing
Tail: Hare's mask guard hairs
Wingcase: Mottled turkey quill
Thorax: Hare's ear dubbing

The Gold-Ribbed Hare's Ear is, perhaps, Idaho's most popular nymph, as evidenced by its presence in every fly bin in the Gem State. When beginning fly tyers take a course and attempt their first nymph, it's likely a Hare's Ear. When beginning fly fishers head astream for the first time, a Hare's Ear might very well be tied to the end of their leader—it's that popular. It's also productive, which is why many sage anglers continue to use the Gold-Ribbed Hare's Ear. As with its cousin—the Flashback Hare's Ear Nymph—the standard Hare's Ear matches mayfly nymphs nicely. It can be fished in rivers and lakes with equal success.

Golden Stone Nymph

See color photo	**Hook:** Daiichi 1710, 2X-long, sizes 8, 10
	Thread: Brown
	Body: Golden olive crystal chenille
	Thorax: Natural brown hare's ear
	Tail: Golden goose biots
Head: Beadhead	

Created by Jack Parker of Idaho Falls in the late 1980s to early 1990s, the Golden Stone Nymph is particularly effective on the Big Lost River, where stoneflies are present from late May through August. It is best tied in sizes 8 and 10.

"You can fish that pattern from opening day through summer because the river is full of golden stoneflies," said Greg Webster, who runs The Bent Rod Sports Shop in Mackay. "During the early season, the stoneflies are large, but by August they are mostly comprised of the little Yellow Sally, so you have to change sizes as the season progresses. We typically dead-drift the pattern, but it takes fish as it swings through the shallows, too."

Green Butt Skunk (steelhead fly)

Hook: TMC 7999, sizes 0, 2

Thread: Black

Wing: White calf tail

Tail: Red hackle fibers

Butt: Fluorescent green chenille

Rib: Fine silver oval tinsel

Body: Black chenille

Hackle: Black

A CLASSIC WINTER PATTERN along the Pacific Coast, the Green Butt Skunk is a producer in Idaho, too, especially when worked through off-color water. During thin-water periods (typically fall conditions on the Clearwater) the skunk can be tied without weight and with small chenille, which produces a modest silhouette.

Gulper Special (mayfly)

Hook: TMC 100, sizes 14–22

Thread: Brown

Body: Brown, olive, or tan rabbit

Tail: Grizzly hackle fibers

Hackle: Grizzly hackle

Wing: Post of white, orange, or black poly yarn

THIS FLY IS SYNONYMOUS WITH MONTANA'S Hebgen Reservoir and its sizable rainbow and brown trout, which have come to be known simply as "gulpers." Many eastern Idaho fly-fishers travel north, just past West Yellowstone, when they hear, "The gulpers are going at Hebgen."

The Gulper Special, which was created by Al Troth of Dillon, Montana, is very similar to the Parachute Adams except that the Gulper Special sports a poly yarn post in various colors. The post is highly visible, even in choppy conditions. A white or orange post is an excellent choice on sunny days. A black post shows up nicely on overcast days.

Hair-Wing Dun (mayfly)

Hook:	TMC 900BL, sizes 10–14
Thread:	Olive
Rib:	Brown floss
Tail:	Black moose hair, split
Hackle:	Grizzly and grizzly dyed olive
Body:	Olive Antron or Superfine Dubbing
Wing:	Deer hair

ANGLERS CAN FISH THIS PATTERN in a number of sizes to match many mayfly species, but the Hair-Wing Dun is my top choice when matching large Green Drake mayflies, which emerge on many of Idaho's tailwater and freestone streams.

One of the best hatches occurs on the Big Wood River in mid-July, just as receding runoff allows brave waders their first shot at the river. Dressed with flotant, the Hair-Wing Dun rides high and is visible in choppy water, especially in bright light. Fish this pattern throughout the river, including tiny side channels, which often hold large trout during the early season.

Halfback Emerger (PMD, mayfly)

Hook: TMC 5210, sizes 16, 18	
Thread: Brown	
Tail: Brown or gold Z-Lon	See color photo
Rib: Fine copper wire	
Abdomen: Pheasant tail fibers	
Wing Case: Deer hair	
Thorax: Yellow Superfine Dubbing	
Head: Yellow Superfine Dubbing	

MIKE LAWSON DESIGNED THE HALFBACK EMERGER to match crippled Pale Morning Duns, which are most evident on spring creeks and tailwaters during late summer.

"It works especially well when the air temperature is high," said Lawson. "At that time, there is a higher mortality of mayfly duns. This pattern, with only its wing case pushing through the surface film, takes advantage of the fish sitting just under the surface with a limited sight range."

Lawson stresses that this pattern should have a buoyant wing case. "If you use deer hair or elk hair, use a clump so it almost looks like a Humpy. The other option is to use closed-cell foam. It probably works a little better than the hair."

Halloween Leech (streamer)

Hook: Dai-Riki 700 or 710, sizes 2, 4, 6, 8	
Head: Black bead	
Thread: Black monocord	See color photo
Tail: Burnt orange marabou	
Hackle: Grizzly dyed orange or olive	
Body: Variegated burnt orange and black chenille	

WHEN FLY PATTERNS AND FISHING TECHNIQUES for eastern Idaho's tremendous trout factory, called Henry's Lake, are brought up in conversation, Bill Schiess is always mentioned.

Schiess ran B. S. Flies, located on the lake's eastern shore, for many years. He authored the book *Fishing Henry's Lake*, and developed many effective lake patterns over the years. Perhaps no fly fisher has spent more time on Henry's Lake than Schiess.

One of Schiess' best creations, the Halloween Leech, is a standby at Henry's Lake, and it has proved effective on all of Idaho's still waters.

Hare's Ear Rubber Leg Nymph

See photo of
Gold-Ribbed
Hare's Ear

Hook: VMC 7071 or Daiichi 1560, sizes 4–18

Thread: Brown or black Cascade Supreme

Body: Blend of hare's mask and gray squirrel tail underfur. This should be coarse and with lots of guard hairs

Legs: Square rubber dyed pinkish tan. The first pair of legs are tied in at the junction of the body and thorax and are swept back. The second pair of legs are tied in just behind the hook eye and are swept back

Thorax: Mottled oak turkey

Tail: Two strands of rubber dyed pinkish tan

Weight: .015 lead wire for sizes 10 though 16; .020 for sizes 4 through 8

Rib: Gold oval tinsel; fine on sizes 10 through 16, and medium on sizes 4 through 8

THIS WARREN SCHOTH VARIATION of the standard Hare's Ear Nymph, along with many other variations, is becoming increasingly available at western fly shops, which is a testament to its effectiveness.

"It's a good year-round pattern because it has all the attributes of a mayfly nymph and it's also taken as a caddis," Schoth said. "When tied in the larger sizes, it's also a good match for the larger stoneflies. The rubber legs just give it more motion than the standard pattern offers."

Hatch Master (mayfly)

Hook: Mustad 94838, sizes 16–22	
Tail, Body, and Wing: Constructed from one mallard breast feather	See color photo
Hackle: Color to match insect	

SOUTH-CENTRAL IDAHO'S SILVER CREEK holds some very large trout, but it's one of the most difficult waters in the world on which to set the hook on a good fish. The trout in "the Creek," as it is called locally, are terribly wary and incredibly selective: They'll bolt downstream if they glimpse the shadow of a line, and they'll inspect flies like a nuclear physicist glaring through a microscope at the INEEL (Idaho Nuclear Engineering and Environmental Laboratory).

Silver Creek demands precisely tied flies, and one of the best early mayfly patterns was the Hatch Master, created by Dick Alfs, who ran the first fly shop in Sun Valley, Idaho.

Alfs' pattern, which hammers fish during mayfly emergences, is tied with a single dyed mallard breast feather whose quill extends off the shank of the hook. Much of the quill is then cut away, which creates a split-tail design. The rest of the feather is then pulled forward and tied to the hook. The tips are tied up to form the wing. A stiff hackle, wrapped behind and in front of the wing, finishes the fly. Because of its realistic impression and the ease with which it is tied, the Hatch Master should have a place in the fly box of every angler who fishes Silver Creek.

John Huber, a guide for Lost River Outfitters is an advocate of the Hatch Master. "It's tied to imitate all the mayflies—PMDs, Green Drakes, Tricos, Mahogany Duns, and *Baetis*," Huber said. "I especially like to fish it during *Baetis* hatches. I tie the fly on with a Duncan Loop, which allows that extended body to wiggle back and forth in the surface film just like a natural. It's definitely one of the top flies for Silver Creek."

Hemingway Caddis

Hook: TMC 100, sizes 14, 16, 18

Thread: Olive

Body: Olive Superfine Dubbing palmered with medium dun hackle

Wing: Mallard quill

Underwing: Wood duck mallard flank

Thorax: Peacock herl

Hackle: Medium dun

THIS FLY WAS DERIVED FROM the Henryville Special, which Mike Lawson tied commercially for a fly shop in Michigan during the early 1970s. Lawson changed the body color and the profile of the wing to match many of the dark caddis species he encounters on his home waters of eastern Idaho.

"We didn't know what to call the fly, but Jack Hemingway was really impressed with it and he fished it often, so we just called it the Hemingway Caddis," Lawson said. "The fly is hackled heavy enough that you can dead-drift it or skate it. I like to fish a caddis pupa off it as a dropper."

Lawson says the Hemingway Caddis works best during the early season, from late April through mid-July, when eastern Idaho sees most of its caddis activity.

Henry's Fork Golden Stone
and Henry's Fork Salmon Fly (stoneflies)

Henry's Fork Golden Stone

Hook: TMC 5262, sizes 6, 8, 10

Thread: Tan

Tail: Dark tan elk

Hackle: Brown palmered, trimmed on bottom

Body: Light elk hair

Wing: Light elk hair

Head: Dark elk, bullet-head style

Henry's Fork Salmon Fly

Hook: TMC 5262, sizes 2, 4, 6

Thread: Fire orange

Tail: Dark moose

Hackle: Brown, palmered and trimmed

Body: Burnt orange elk hair

Wing: Dark elk hair

Head: Black elk hair, bullet-head style

See photo of Henry's Fork Golden Stone

DUE TO THEIR AERODYNAMIC DESIGN, these patterns are easy to cast and, like Lawson's Henry's Fork Hopper, they provide a realistic silhouette on the water. When fishing the Henry's Fork early in the season, these are two patterns you do not want to be without.

"A stonefly sits pretty low on the water and these patterns match that," creator Mike Lawson said. "The Henry's Fork has prolific hatches of golden stoneflies and salmon flies all the way downstream to St. Anthony, with the exception of the flat-water stretch through the Ranch. Typically, salmon flies come off the last week of May and the first week of June, with the golden stones coming off a week later. What is interesting about the golden stones is that they continue to hatch well into July in Box Canyon, and that is much later than you see on most Idaho rivers. They just keep dribbling along and the fish look for them."

Henry's Fork Hopper (terrestrial)

Hook: TMC 5212, sizes 4, 6

Thread: Yellow

Body: Cream elk rump, reverse-style, extended

Underwing: Yellow elk hair

Overwing: Mottled brown hen pheasant saddle feather coated with Dave's Flexament

Head: Gray elk, bullet-head style

Legs: White or yellow rubber

See color photo

ANOTHER MIKE LAWSON CREATION, this hopper is one of the most effective terrestrial patterns when fishing Idaho's spring creeks and still waters.

Due to its construction, this pattern sits low in the water, like a natural, and is apt to draw even the wariest trout up for inspection.

"Really, this was my first pattern and I started tying it in 1971 when there weren't a lot of hopper patterns on the market," Lawson said. "At that time, the only hopper pattern that had ever worked for me was a pattern described by Vince Marinaro in *A Modern Dry Fly Code*. That hopper is tied with a quill stem body. The bottom tip of a turkey's quill is hollow and Marinaro cut it, then covered it with epoxy. That pattern was very effective, so I studied its silhouette in my aquarium. Then I looked at real hoppers, which enlightened me: The real hoppers float way down in the surface film like an iceberg. Some float with more body below the surface than above. I looked at all the commercial hopper patterns available and they did not look right at all. They looked great from above, but not below. The Marinaro hopper looked great, but it was so intricate to tie that it was virtually impossible.

"I tried to match that hopper, but I used deer and elk hair instead of turkey quill," Lawson added. "Originally I reversed the hair and segmented it with thread, but I clipped the hair to form a head. Now, I go with a bullet-head style and it looks more realistic, plus it's more aerodynamic. I've also added legs to the pattern, which makes it a little more realistic looking. Today, foam works great for the body, too. If you don't want to deal with the deer or elk hair, go with the foam.

"You can do a lot with this pattern," Lawson said. "You can skip it off the surface so it lands under undercut banks. Because of its aerodynamic design, you can drive it into the wind, when some of the best hopper fishing occurs. It's also an effective pattern for bass and, especially, panfish. A lot of guys in Texas fish my hopper pattern."

Henry's Fork Yellow Sally (stonefly)

Hook: TMC 5262, size 16

Thread: Yellow

Tail: Medium dun hackle fibers

Abdomen: Yellow Antron

Wing: Elk hair

Hackle: Medium dun, clipped top and bottom

Thorax: Yellow Antron

HERE'S A PATTERN THAT'S EXTREMELY EFFECTIVE on Idaho's rivers, but is often overlooked by anglers. Rarely do fly fishers harbor specific Yellow Sally patterns in their fly boxes; instead, most choose to match the insect with an Elk Hair Caddis or a yellow Humpy. According to Mike Lawson, who created this pattern, that is a mistake.

"I am surprised there aren't more patterns to specifically imitate this group of stoneflies, because they can be really prolific," Lawson said. "When the fish are selectively feeding on Yellow Sallies, an Elk Hair Caddis does not offer the right silhouette. Those stoneflies are long and slender and they float low in the water.

"I tie my pattern with a longer-shank hook, and the wing is tied fairly low," Lawson said. "The one common characteristic you find on all the Yellow Sally patterns is they are all tied with a red butt to represent an egg sac. Often the trout do feed on those females with an egg sac, but not always. Sometimes they seem to focus on those without the egg sac. You can tie some with red butts and some without, or you can be lazy like me and tie them all without and just doctor a few with a red permanent felt-tip pen."

Occasionally, an angler may not find many Yellow Sallies present, but don't think the fish aren't looking for them. When they are keyed in on Sallies, they'll come up for a size-16 imitation whether or not any naturals are present.

"You can always tell if some Sallies have been around

because you will find their shucks all over the rocks near shore," Lawson said. "For that reason, this fly is a great searching pattern."

Horsethief Leech (streamer)

Hook: Streamer hook, sizes 10, 12	
Thread: Brown or black	
Tail: Brown marabou	
Body: Canadian brown mohair	

See color photo

THE HORSETHIEF LEECH WAS DESIGNED to match leeches at Horsethief Reservoir, and that's where the pattern works best.

Marv Taylor, who created this pattern, nosed around Horsethief long enough to notice that the trout homed in on small brown leeches.

"Horsethief has a large population of very small dark brown leeches," Taylor said. "A Canadian Brown Mohair works there, but the Horsethief Leech is more appropriate and it catches more fish. I tie it in size 10 and 12."

Idanha Yellow Jacket (terrestrial)

See color photo

Hook: Daiichi 1280, sizes 8, 10, 12

Thread: Yellow 3/0 monocord

Underbody: Yellow closed-cell foam

Tail: Red saddle hackle fibers (preferred) or red-dyed deer hair

Body: Bright yellow rayon floss

Rib: Black rayon floss (waxed). Use tighter spirals as you move forward toward the thorax

Wing: Furnace hackle tips

Thorax: Black rayon floss

Hackle: Furnace wound through thorax

WARREN SCHOTH UPDATED THIS OLD PATTERN, which was originally tied and fished in northern Utah and eastern

Idaho during the dust bowl years, when yellow jackets and wasps were abundant.

"We brought this fly back during the last series of drought years when there were lots of yellow jackets and wasps working the exposed mud banks along the rivers and the edges of lakes," Schoth said. "I have a fondness for old fly patterns and this one works, especially when fished along lake margins or those mud banks. It was originally designed to swing through the water, but it sits low enough that you can fish it dead-drift if you want to."

Schoth may have remembered this pattern when he was stung by yellow jackets—180 times!—when fishing Washington's Pass Lake.

"About twenty-five of them hit me in the nuts," Schoth recalled. "They just flew up my pant legs, so I jumped in the lake. I didn't have any epinephrine with me and I was swelling up badly. Plus, I could barely breathe. A game warden came by and rushed me to Anacortes, where a doctor met me. They gave me epinephrine and I started to breathe again, but I was still whimpering like a dog. If that warden hadn't come by and called ahead for a doctor to meet us (it was a Sunday), I would have died."

Improved Sofa Pillow (stonefly)

Hook: TMC 200R, sizes 2, 4	
Thread: Black or orange	
Tail: Elk hair	
Body: Orange poly yarn or Antron	
Rib: Fine gold wire	
Wing: Elk hair	
Hackle: Palmered furnace over body; brown over thorax	

AS MENTIONED IN CHAPTER ONE, the Sofa Pillow was created in the 1940s by Pat and Sig Barnes who operated Pat Barnes Tackle Shop in West Yellowstone, Montana. The

Improved Sofa Pillow uses an elk-hair wing and tail, rather than the red squirrel tail that is used in the classic dressing.

The Improved Sofa Pillow is a great match for Idaho's giant *Pteronarcys* stonefly hatches, and it doubles as a golden stonefly imitation when those species are present. Particularly effective on large, choppy rivers, the Improved Sofa Pillow excels on such waters as the Henry's Fork, the South Fork Snake, and the South Fork Boise.

Integration (streamer)

Hook: Mustad 79580, sizes 2–10

Thread: Black

Body: Thick silver tinsel

Underwing: White bucktail (under hook shank)

Overwing: Black bucktail

ONE OF TED TRUEBLOOD'S MOST FAMOUS CREATIONS, the Integration is a good minnow imitation that proves effective on many Idaho waters, especially lakes and reservoirs where trout and bass are found. Trueblood fished this pattern for trout, but he most often cast it on Owyhee Reservoir for bass.

Marv Taylor of Boise, Idaho, who owns an original Ted Trueblood–tied Integration, often adds red bucktail to the head collar of the fly to imitate gills. He ties it in sizes 2 to 10.

J.J. Special (nymph/streamer)

Hook: Mustad 9672, sizes 2–8

Thread: Black monocord

Body: Gold Crystal Chenille or medium brown chenille with a lateral line of Krystal Flash

Underbody: Built with a generous amount of lead

Hackle (optional): Brown saddle or grizzly

Legs: Yellow rubber

Head (optional): Bead

Tail: Brown or black marabou with yellow marabou on each side

THIS UGLY PATTERN WAS CREATED in Jackson Hole, Wyoming, by Jimmy Jones. Because of its effectiveness on large cutthroat trout, it jumped state borders to become a mainstay on Idaho's South Fork Snake River. I've used this fly on rivers in Washington, Oregon, Wyoming, Alaska, and Montana, and its been effective wherever I've fished it—especially for cutthroat and brown trout. It's especially productive on eastern Idaho's brawling brown trout streams. Cast against the bank and stripped toward a drift boat, there may not be a better fly for large fish during the early season, when high water and limited visibility restricts anglers. When using the J.J. Special you can bet the fish are going to see your fly!

Kaufmann's Rubber Leg Stone (nymph)

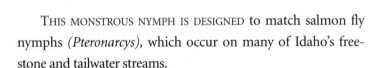

Hook: TMC 300 or 5263, sizes 2–6

Thread: Black

Antennae: Black turkey biots

Tail: Black turkey biots

Rib: Black Swannundaze

Abdomen: Black dubbing

Wing Case: Dark turkey tail, lacquered

Legs: Black rubber

Thorax: Black dubbing

Head: Black dubbing

THIS MONSTROUS NYMPH IS DESIGNED to match salmon fly nymphs *(Pteronarcys),* which occur on many of Idaho's freestone and tailwater streams.

During high water, when salmon flies crawl from midstream boulders to the edge of the stream, a Kaufmann's Rubber Leg Stone often hammers eager nymph-scarfing trout. I dead-drift this pattern near shore. Weighting the fly with wraps of lead helps get the pattern down to the bottom—where it needs to be—in heavy water. This pattern is most effective on large rivers, but it also produces on smaller freestones, such as the Big and Little Wood Rivers.

Lawson's Brown Drake Nymph

Hook: TMC 5262, sizes 10, 12

Thread: Brown

Tail: Brown partridge

Rib: Fine gold wire

Gills: Gray marabou

Abdomen: Light yellowish tan Antron

Legs: Brown partridge

Thorax: Light yellowish tan Antron

"BROWN DRAKE NYMPHS HAVE PROMINENT GILLS, so I tie this pattern with marabou on each side of the hook, wrapped with wire and picked out," said Mike Lawson, who created this nymph to match the Henry's Fork's awesome Brown Drake population.

"I like to fish this pattern with soft twitches of the rod tip. Also, I like to pick a specific fish and try for him. If you just cover the water here with this nymph, you will only catch whitefish. You need to study the rises, pick out the trout, then try to swing this nymph in front of a fish."

That's good advice to follow when fishing this pattern: Lawson landed his largest Henry's Fork rainbow (in the Railroad Ranch section) on the Brown Drake Nymph. The fish measured 25 inches, and was released. Lawson admitted, "I thought I was casting to a whitefish."

Lawson's Floating Nymph (Baetis/mayfly)

Hook: TMC 100, sizes 16, 18, 20

Thread: Olive

Tail: Light blue dun hackle fibers

Abdomen: *Baetis* Superfine Dubbing

Wing: Light gray ball of poly dubbing

Thorax: *Baetis* Superfine Dubbing

Legs: Blue dun hackle fibers

THIS PATTERN SPRUNG FROM MIKE LAWSON'S insect studies in his home aquarium. Anglers can tie this pattern to match a variety of mayflies, but Lawson insists that it best matches tiny *Baetis,* which are present on Idaho's streams and still waters from mid-September through November.

"I watched a lot of flies in my aquarium, and most drift on the surface for quite a while until they get their wings unrolled," Lawson said. "I think the fish key on the low profile they provide at that time. The poly ball represents the wing case unfurling."

Lawson's Foam Beetle (terrestrial)

Hook: TMC 100, sizes 12, 14, 16	
Thread: Black	
Back: Black foam	
Underbody: Peacock herl	
Legs: Black rubber	
Indicator: Orange or yellow yarn	

THIS PATTERN CLOSELY RESEMBLES a dozen or more effective beetle patterns. No matter which pattern you choose, it makes sense to carry a few beetles in your fly box. During late summer and early fall, a beetle can draw strikes after morning mayfly emergences and spinner falls when all other patterns fail. A beetle imitation, in general, is a good hatch breaker, a fly even selectively feeding fish might eat.

Lawson's Green Drake Paradrake (mayfly)

Hook: TMC 900BL, sizes 10, 12	
Thread: Olive or yellow	See color photo
Wing: Dark gray elk hair, yellow calf tail, or black moose hair	
Tail: Moose	
Body: Olive elk tied extended-body style	
Hackle: Grizzly dyed olive	

DOUG SWISHER AND CARL RICHARDS introduced this pattern in their book, *Selective Trout*. Mike Lawson refined the Green Paradrake to make it as effective as possible. And he's had at his disposal one of the best testing grounds in the world: the Henry's Fork of the Snake River.

"The first Paradrakes were kind of bulky," Lawson said. "I tie a version that is much more streamlined and maybe a little easier to tie. In fact, you tie it in the bullet-head style but you don't clip the hair. Instead, you just bring it all the way back past the hook shank and form the extended body."

Although the Paradrake looks intimidating to tie, it's not a difficult pattern to master. However, Lawson offers this advice: "Don't make the body too long. Almost all the commercially tied Paradrakes I see are too long. The body should be no more than half the hook shank long. If it's any longer, it throws a completely unrealistic silhouette. Also, if it's tied too long, that big extension causes an angler to miss a lot of strikes. This pattern is very effective when tied right, but it's easy to screw up."

The best days to fish the Green Paradrake are when the weather is overcast or rainy and those big insects must ride the surface for extended periods until their wings dry. During those conditions, trout absolutely crush them.

This pattern can also be tied in tan or brown and fished during the Brown Drake emergence.

Lawson's Hen Spinner (Slate Olive) (mayfly)

Hook: TMC 100, sizes 16–22	
Thread: Olive	
Wing: Light dun hen hackle tips, tied spent-wing style	
Tail: Medium dun hackle fibers, split	

Body: Olive Superfine Dubbing

Note: This pattern can be tied to match PMDs, Tricos, and *Callibaetis*

SELECTED FLIES FROM BEST FLIES FOR IDAHO

Bing's Hopper

Extended-Body Olive Dun

Fifi

Golden Stone Nymph

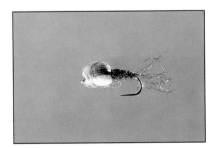

Halfback Emerger

Halloween Leech

Hatch Master

Henry's Fork Hopper

Horsethief Leech

Idanha Yellow Jacket

Lawson's Green Drake Paradrake

LC Moose

Lempke's Salmon Fly

Little Jewel

Loop-Wing Dun

Mackay Special

Marabou Jughead

Marcella's Trout Fly

Master Nymph (Epoxy)

The Meat-Getter

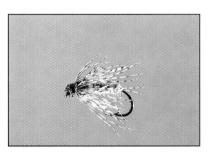

Moss Caddis Emerger

Otter Nymph

Philo Betto

Renegade

Sadie Thompson Woolly Bugger

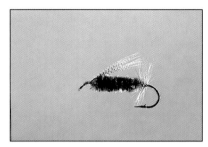

Sheep Creek Special

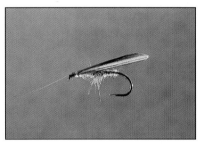

Slow Water Caddis

Spent Partridge Caddis

Stan's Willow Fly

Stayner's Ducktail

Taylor Shrimp

Trude

THIS PATTERN WAS INTRODUCED by Doug Swisher and Carl Richards, but Mike Lawson found the original too bulky and made it more streamlined.

"Spinners are much more streamlined than duns and it is tough to get that impression if you tie this pattern with a ball of fur to split the tails, like Swisher and Richards do. I don't split the tails with that fur because it adds too much bulk to the pattern. Instead, I just flare some hackle fibers, and that allows me to keep that nice delicate taper."

The pattern was originally tied with hen hackle tips, but Lawson encourages tyers to use modern materials or feathers from wild birds.

"Clear Antron works well for the wing, but I like [Hungarian] partridge hackle tips best because they are gray and have a natural speckle to them. Spinners can be hard to see on the water so, often, I put one wrap of hackle behind, and one in front of the wing. Then I clip the bottom of the hackle so I maintain contact with the surface, but I can see the hackle above the water. That works especially well when matching the large mayflies, like Green and Brown Drakes."

LC Moose (stonefly)

Hook: Mustad 9672, sizes 2, 4, 6	
Thread: Bright orange floss or waxed nylon	See color
Body: Orange or black elk hair	photo
Tail: Black or gray elk hair tips	
Rib: Brown saddle hackle	
Hackle: Dark brown or gray dun saddle hackle	
Legs (optional): Black rubber	
Wing: Moose mane	
Collar: Dark brown saddle hackle	

REXBURG, IDAHO, OFFERS FLY TYERS great opportunity to test creative stonefly patterns: The Henry's Fork, the South Fork Snake, the Teton, the Falls, and the Warm Rivers, as well as Robinson Creek, all have good hatches, at different times, of giant *Pteronarcys* and golden stoneflies.

Steve Christensen and Wendell Lewis, fly-tying dentists from Rexburg, took advantage of their geographical locale to thoroughly test stonefly patterns, and their best offering is the LC Moose. When the LC Moose is tied with a dark elk-hair underbody, which also forms the tail, it accurately depicts a female stonefly with an egg sac. The wing is a combination of highly buoyant elk hair and moose mane. The optional legs, which seem to drive large trout crazy, are tied in front of the wing, and are then covered with dark brown or gray dun saddle hackle. The result is a high-floating salmon fly or golden stonefly imitation that offers the added attraction of rubber legs.

Lempke's Salmon Fly (stonefly)

See color photo	**Hook:** TMC 5263, sizes 2, 4
	Thread: Black
	Tail: Dark elk hair tied along the entire hook shank to form an underbody
	Rib: Orange thread

Body: Cassette tape over toothpick, then lacquered

Wing: Light and dark elk hair, mixed

Hackle: Grizzly and brown, trimmed on the underside

THIS PATTERN RIDES LOW IN THE WATER, yet has a heavy wing and hackle so it's visible at a distance. You might at first feel you are fishing with a swallow pattern rather than something that imitates an insect. However, the trout have no reservations when they sight this hapless fly on the water: They pound it.

This pattern works well on all of Idaho's salmon fly waters, and many of my fishing partners have had particular success casting this bug under the willows and overhanging cottonwood limbs that surround the South Fork Boise. Tied tight, this pattern is extremely durable and will bring many trout to the net before you need to change flies.

Light Cahill (mayfly)

Hook: TMC 900 BL, sizes 16, 18, 20

Thread: Pale yellow

Wing: Mallard flank dyed to look like wood duck, upright and divided

Tail: Ginger or cream hackle fibers

Body: Ginger or cream Superfine

Hackle: Ginger or cream

THE LIGHT CAHILL, AN EASTERN PATTERN that was created by Dan Cahill in the 1880s, successfully crossed the continent, and has become a mainstay in Idaho, if not the entire West. Tied in sizes 16 and 18, the Light Cahill is an excellent selection when matching Pale Morning Duns, Pink Alberts, and other light-colored mayflies. You may find, as I have, that this pattern is equally effective on small streams, large rivers, and even spring creeks.

Light Variant (mayfly)

Hook: Mustad 94840, sizes 14–18

Thread: Cream

Wings: Ginger hackle hen tips, upright and divided

Tail: Three elk hairs

Body: Cream dubbing

Hackle: Cream and ginger

THIS PATTERN WAS CREATED by Roy Donnelly, and it is extremely effective in the waters surrounding Jackson Hole, Wyoming, including Yellowstone National Park. A variation of the immensely popular and productive Light Cahill, the Light Variant hit Idaho's waters in the 1950s and quickly drew praise for its excellent buoyancy and visibility.

Wherever it was fished, the Light Variant produced.

The pattern's buoyancy results from its hackle-tip wings: Unlike traditional mallard-flank wings, the wings of the Light Variant are tied upright and divided. When mayflies are present, especially light-colored varieties such as Pale Morning Duns and Pink Alberts, the Light Variant in sizes 14 to 18 is an excellent choice.

Little Jewel (caddisfly)

See color photo	**Hook:** Mustad 9672, 3X-long, sizes 6, 8, 10
	Thread: Black
	Abdomen: Dark olive green chenille
	Rib: Fine gold wire
	Hackle: Furnace hackle trimmed top and bottom

Thorax: Black chenille

Note: Can be tied in variety of colors

THIS PATTERN WAS CREATED by Marv Taylor at Jewel Lake, near Sandpoint, Idaho, but it works on any lake or reservoir where large caddis are present. Crane Falls Reservoir and Horsethief Reservoir are just two examples.

"I tie this pattern to imitate the big caddis that we see at Jewel Lake," Taylor said. "When I first fished there, a friend asked me what I was getting them on and I didn't know what to say. We were fishing Jewel Lake, so that's what I called the fly."

Loop-Wing Dun (PMD)

See color photo	**Hook:** Partridge L3A, sizes 18–24
	Thread: Tan or yellow
	Body: Monofilament and chartreuse Antron yarn (wound)
	Wing: Fine monofilament

Tail: Fine monofilament

Hackle: Medium blue dun

THIS PATTERN IS A BRUCE STAPLES CREATION, but he credits Bing Lempke for the extended-body idea. However, it was Staple's idea to use monofilament for the wing, body-beam, and tail.

"You can tie this pattern in the appropriate size and color to match any of the mayfly duns," Staples said. "I developed this pattern because I thought that many of the mayfly dun patterns had an inferior, heavy wing. By using monofilament for the wing you get a light, suggestive wing that works well."

Mackay Special (cranefly)

Hook: Daiichi 1710, 2X-long, sizes 4, 6, 8

Thread: Orange or brown

Body: Reddish brown or sandy horse mane

Belly: Yellow, green, or orange heavy thread or embroidery floss (split to three strands) woven into body

See color photo

Hackle: Brown or ginger neck woven into body

Wings: Horse hair, tied upright and divided

Head: Build heavy thread head so wings do not push forward

Note: Body, hackle, and belly are woven Potts-fashion

ACE SHINDERLING OF MACKAY, IDAHO, created this killer pattern in the mid-1940s. Most often fished as a cranefly imitation, it also is considered a great attractor pattern. A standby for fly fishers on the Big Lost River, today the Mackay Special is tied by few people due to its fairly complicated weave. Greg Webster, who runs The Bent Rod Sports Shop in Mackay, is one person who ties the fly correctly. Hence, he sells 150 dozen or more Mackay Specials each year.

"If you really want to catch big fish, this is a good fly," Webster said. "I've seen fish to seven pounds taken out of the Big Lost on that fly, so it's a mouthful for the fish.

"It's most often fished as a cranefly imitation, skated across the surface," Webster added. "You may only see a dozen or so craneflies a day on the water, but the fish key in on them. They are tremendously effective on the Big Lost, but guys do well with them on the beaver ponds in Copper Basin, too. Some of the old-timers put weight on the leader above the fly and bounce it along the bottom."

Craneflies are most prominent on the Big Lost between mid-July and mid-September, and a size-6 or -8 Mackay Special best imitates the actual insect. When tied in larger sizes and skated across the surface, the Mackay Special is also effective for Clearwater River steelhead. One of the most appealing aspects to this fly is its durability. As Greg Webster pointed out, "The hook will rust before the weave comes undone."

Magic Perch (streamer)

Hook: VMC 7070 or Daiichi 1720, 3X-long, sizes 2, 4

Thread: Black Cascade Supreme, 0/6 or 0/8

Rib: Waxed 3/0 black monocord

Tail: Orange saddle with orange Crystal hair

Weight: .015 lead wire

Body: Riverborn New Age Chenille in "fools gold" coloration

Wing: Mallard flank dyed medium olive green

Underwing: Black pearlescent Cascade Fly Flash

Hackle: Hot orange saddle hackle and orange Crystal Hair

SOMEWHAT SIMILAR TO RUEL STAYNER'S supremely effective Ducktail, the Magic Perch is colored closer to the natural.

"I developed this pattern over fifteen or twenty years while fishing Magic Reservoir," said Warren Schoth. "Some of those days I fished with Stayner, and we found that this fly is a good color substitute for the Stayner Ducktail, especially in bright light conditions. Perch fry are most prominent at Magic Reservoir during spring, but this pattern works year-round. It's most effective in late May and again when the reservoir drops and the perch fry move to the rocky shoreline areas.

"I like to fish this pattern off a slow sinking line right along the rocks where those perch hang out. It's a decent searching pattern, but it works best when you concentrate on those rocky areas. I use the countdown method to retrieve it. Usually, I start by counting it to the bottom then work my way through the various planes of water. I use a jerk-and-twist retrieve: a 6- to 8-inch pull, and then the twist, with no hesitation. The other technique is to work the shoreline in a float tube and angle your casts tight to the rock banks. Strip three or four times quick, then let it sit. Strip three or four more times and if you don't get hit, pick up the line and crack it back in there."

Malad Ant (terrestrial)

Hook: VMC 7061 or Daiichi 1100, sizes 10–14

Thread: Rusty brown

Body: Burnt or hot orange center between two joints of black-dyed ostrich herl (black-dyed peacock is preferred, but it's hard to find)

Hackle: Dark ginger variant

Wing: Reddish brown Hereford calf tail

Tail: Golden pheasant

Rib: Extra-fine gold rib over center section

THIS WARREN SCHOTH TRUDE-STYLE creation is a solid attractor pattern that passes as a flying ant or grasshopper.

"I fished this fly for twenty years and finally brought it into commercial production," Schoth said. "I developed it on the Malad, but it's worked on all types of waters as far away as New York, and the Deschutes River in Oregon. The three best sizes are 10, 12, and 14."

Marabou Damsel

Hook: TMC 200R, sizes 6 and 8	
Thread: Olive	
Tail: Olive marabou	
Body: Olive marabou	
Rib: Fine copper wire	

Wing: Olive marabou

Head: Beaded chain if desired

THE MARABOU DAMSEL IS A POPULAR, effective damselfly imitation that is super easy to tie—proficient fly-tyers can pump out a dozen or more of these in an hour. This patterns works especially well on lowland lakes and reservoirs, such as Henry's Lake, Island Park Reservoir, and Magic Reservoir, but it also takes fish from moving water, such as Silver Creek and the Henry's Fork. If you don't have any time to spare and you need a few damsel patterns for your fly box, try this tie.

Marabou Jughead (streamer)

See color photo	**Hook:** Mustad 79580, sizes 2, 4, 6, 8
	Thread: Red monocord
	Body: Gold or silver Sparkle Braid
	Weight: Split shot crimped to the hook shank
	Wing: Marabou with strands of Flashabou or

Krystal Flash

Head and Collar: Deer body hair, spun and clipped to shape

THIS POPULAR BRUCE STAPLES CREATION is notable for its ability to reach the bottoms of rivers, where eastern Idaho's largest brown trout dwell (Staples says the pattern is one of the best for reaching bottom when using heavy leaders). This pattern is most effective when retrieved in quick strips, a tactic that mimics an escaping sculpin. This pattern is also suggestive of a drifting leech or earthworm.

Marcella's Trout Fly (stonefly)

Hook: Mustad 9672, sizes 2, 4, 6

Thread: Black nylon

Tail: Elk hair

Rib: Brown saddle hackle

Body: Orange or red yarn

Wing: Brown bucktail

Hackle: Furnace hackles

See color photo

A SALMON FLY IMITATION CREATED by Marcella Oswald of Idaho Falls, Marcella's Trout Fly grew immensely popular in the 1950s and 1960s. Due to demand, Oswald tied hundreds of dozens of them each year. Dressed bushy, Oswald's pattern rides high, is visible in heavy water, and is durable.

Marv's Fly (damselfly)

Hook: Streamer hook, sizes 10, 12

Thread: Light olive Danville thread

Tail: Light olive or gold marabou

Hackle: Grizzly dyed light olive or gold and trimmed short

Body: Light olive variegated chenille (small)

Gills: Light olive marabou

CONTRARY TO WHAT MANY MODERN FLY TYERS believe, simple, suggestive patterns do catch fish. Eyes, elbows, and "arseholes," as some western dudes might say, are not required for success.

"I think the reason why the Marv's Fly is such an excellent pattern is because it's just very suggestive of a damsel nymph," said Marv Taylor, who created the pattern. "There are a lot of damsel nymphs on the market that copy the actual insect to a tee. They have wing cases, the legs are just right, eyes. . . . My philosophy is that sometimes those patterns don't even work as well as the less sophisticated ones. I would have to have the mind of a trout to tell you exactly why that is. All any of us can do when developing flies and techniques to fish them is to use them over and over until we get something that really works well and that is when you can say you have a good fly. The Marv's Fly has proven itself as a great damsel imitation.

"I fish the Marv's fly unweighted, off a sinking line with a short leader," Taylor added. "If the fish are taking it for a damsel I use a hand-twist retrieve with maybe a few twitches. You want that fly to wiggle through the water."

Taylor notes that most fly shops sell chenille that's too large for the Marv's Fly. Taylor uses size-1 or -01, small chenille. With that material he achieves the slender build of the natural damselfly nymph.

Marv's Halloween Fly (streamer)

See color photo of Halloween Leech	**Hook:** Dai-Riki 700 or 710, sizes 4, 6, 8, 10
	Thread: Black
	Body: Orange and black chenille
	Tail: Black marabou
	Hackle: Grizzly hackle dyed orange

THIS PATTERN, ALSO KNOWN AS the Anderson Ranch Leech, closely resembles Bill Schiess' Halloween Fly, which gained prominence on Henry's Lake. The only true difference is that Marv's Halloween Fly, created by Marv Taylor of Boise, uses a standard orange coloration instead of burnt orange.

"This pattern hasn't made its mark yet, but it's a good one and I think, eventually, it will be widely used," Taylor said. "It really hasn't done anything for me at Henry's Lake, but I fished it a lot at Anderson Ranch Reservoir in the late 1980s and early 1990s when the reservoir was low and there were lots of big rainbows around—fish to seven or eight pounds.

"We found those fish chasing kokanee up the creeks and

we fished deep for them, in 10 to 20 feet of water," Taylor added. "We just scratched the bottom for them and I am sure those fish took the fly for a crawdad. Really, we fly-fishers don't fish crawdads enough and there is a lack of patterns to imitate them. Fish understand that that crustacean is so nutritious they can't let them pass by. But nobody fishes a crawdad pattern because they have to be right on the bottom and that is difficult to do."

Master Nymph (Epoxy) (PMD)

Hook: VMC 7070 or Daiichi 1720, 3X-long, sizes 12–20

Thread: Rusty brown

Body: Rabbit and Antron blend, dark rust brown

Overbody: Dark mottled turkey coated with epoxy or Dave's Flexament

Hackle: Brown partridge (four strands per side)

Median Line: White Uni-Thread

Tail: Three reddish brown cock pheasant tail fibers widely separated

Thorax: Dark rust brown to match body

Wing Case: Dark mottled turkey with drop of epoxy (epoxy must be raised/do not foul legs with epoxy)

Rib: Extra fine copper wire

Gills: Tan marabou

Weight: .010 lead wire, flattened

See color photo

THIS VARIATION OF THE EPOXY NYMPH was developed by Warren Schoth in the mid-1990s. Schoth reports that this pattern, which can be adapted to match any mayfly species in Idaho, is superb wherever it is fished.

"It's just a good general nymph that works good wherever you find PMDs," Schoth said. "I adapted it from [Ernest] Schwiebert's book *Nymphs,* and it's worked all over the West."

The Meat-Getter (caddisfly)

Hook: Mustad 94838, sizes 14–18	
Thread: Yellow or tan	
Body: Yellow or tan poly yarn	
Wing: Stiff elk or deer hair	

See color photo

CREATED BY BOB BEAN OF BLACKFOOT, IDAHO, the Meat-Getter is a low-riding caddisfly pattern that works especially well in flat sections of tailwaters and spring creeks. Bean tested the pattern on the spring creeks north of American Falls Reservoir—especially those on the Blackfoot/Fort Hall Indian Reservation—but it is equally effective on south-central Idaho's Silver Creek, Billingsley Creek, and the reservation spring creeks. When mayfly emergences compliment caddis activity, the Meat-Getter is an adequate substitute for the Pale Morning Dun.

Mickey Finn (steamer)

Hook: TMC 300, sizes 2, 4	
Thread: Black	
Rib: Fine oval silver tinsel	
Body: Flat silver tinsel	
Wing: Yellow and red bucktail	

I WAS FIRST INTRODUCED TO THIS PATTERN while fishing for king salmon in Alaska. Those fish, brutes to forty-nine pounds that I landed on a six-weight Sage RPL, hammered this pattern. In Idaho there are no longer salmon to chase, but the Mickey Finn is a good pattern to try during fall when brown trout are particularly aggressive. Do they identify the Mickey Finn as a small cutthroat or rainbow diving in for a taste of caviar? I don't know, but I do know this: more than one four-pound-plus brown has swallowed this pattern when I've twisted it to the end of my leader.

Moose Mane Extended-Body Green Drake (mayfly)

Hook: Mustad 9523; Daiichi 1150 or 1140, sizes 10, 12	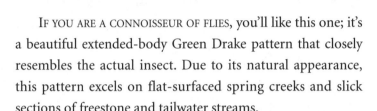
Rib: Sunrise orange embroidery floss	
Body: Western olive Fly-Rite dubbing	
Hackle: Dark bronze or olive dun	
Wing: Dyed yellow or olive hen cape or dyed grizzly hackle tips	
Tail: Two or three strands of moose mane	

IF YOU ARE A CONNOISSEUR OF FLIES, you'll like this one; it's a beautiful extended-body Green Drake pattern that closely resembles the actual insect. Due to its natural appearance, this pattern excels on flat-surfaced spring creeks and slick sections of freestone and tailwater streams.

Dan Curtis designed this fly to match Green Drakes on northern Idaho's Coeur d'Alene River, but the dressing can be adapted to match any mayfly species.

"There is an excellent hatch of Green Drakes on the Coeur d'Alene that extends from the second week of May through mid-June," Curtis said. "I developed the Moose Mane Extended-Body Green Drake to match those insects, and I think it's the most effective pattern around. I've tested other patterns and I find the Moose Mane 60 percent more effective than the others."

Mormon Girl (wet fly)

Hook: Mustad 7957B, sizes 12–16	
Thread: Black nylon	
Wings: Mallard flank tied upright and divided	
Egg Sac: Red floss	
Rib: Silver tinsel	
Body: Yellow dubbing or floss	
Hackle: Brown	

LIKELY DEVELOPED SOMEWHERE IN UTAH in the early 1900s, the Mormon Girl is a productive pattern that should be included in every fly box in the northern Rockies. Tied in sizes 12 through 16, the Mormon Girl is an ideal match for the West's little yellow stoneflies, which are commonly called the Yellow Sally. The most common species in Idaho are *Isoperla* and *Alloperla*; they are present on freestone and tail-water streams beginning in June and extending into September. However, many anglers ignore the opportunity to cast small stonefly imitations when mayflies and caddis-flies hatch in unison. This can be a mistake. Often, trout will key on the awkward, easily captured stonefly even when PMDs and caddis species abound. You're unlikely to find pods of fish steadily sipping stoneflies off the surface, but you can blind cast the Mormon Girl across riffles and choppy runs, where the insects are most dense, with good success. Remember, little yellow stonefly hatches may be locally heavy, especially in those riffled sections. Tied with red floss to suggest an egg sac, the Mormon Girl is extremely effective when skated across riffles or dead-drifted along choppy runs.

Moss Caddis Emerger (soft hackle wet fly)

See color photo	**Hook:** Mustad 7957B, sizes 14–18
	Thread: Black nylon
	Body: Woven green floss
	Thorax: Peacock herl
	Hackle: A few turns of partridge

DEVELOPED BY SCOTT MOSS of Idaho Falls, this pattern is a killer on the Henry's Fork during its early-season caddis blitz, which occurs in the year-round section extending from Ashton Dam downstream to the river's confluence with the main branch of the Snake.

The Moss Caddis Emerger is especially effective when caddisflies struggle to reach the surface. Dead-drift the fly through medium-depth riffles and runs and allow it to swing toward the surface at the end of the drift.

Muddler Minnow (streamer)

Hook: TMC 5263, sizes 2, 4, 6, 8

Thread: Black

Tail: Mottled turkey quill

Body: Gold Diamond Braid or flat tinsel

Underwing: Gray squirrel tail

Wing: Mottled turkey quill

Collar: Spun deer hair

Head: Caribou or deer

Don Gapen of Minnesota created this pattern in the 1950s. It was originally intended to take brook trout in Lake Nipigon, Ontario, but it caught on in Montana and was highly publicized by Dan Bailey's Fly Shop and author Joe Brooks. Today, the Muddler is a standard in western fly bins and it's carried by many of Idaho's most prominent anglers. The Muddler imitates a sculpin, which is common throughout the trout waters of Idaho. Fished off a sink-tip or full-sink line or with the aid of split shot, this pattern is a killer when it dives among the bottom rocks.

N. A. Steelhead Bugger (steelhead fly)

Hook: Daiichi 2441 or TMC 7999, sizes 0–2

Thread: Hot orange

Body: Riverborn New Age Super Chenille, volcano color

Tail: Hot orange and fluorescent orange marabou mixed, with about eight to ten strands of pearl Cascade Crystal Hair

Hackle: Full-spot guinea fowl dyed hot orange

Rib: Hot orange saddle hackle, tied in tip first and palmered forward

Head: Gold bead

Weight: Heavily weighted with .025 lead wire

Here's a steelhead pattern, also known as the Volcano Bugger, that was created by Warren Schoth and is effective wherever it's fished. Alaska, Washington, Oregon, and Idaho—no matter where it's thrown—it seems to draw strikes.

"It's especially effective on Idaho's Clearwater and Salmon Rivers," Schoth said. "It can be fished through the full season, but we sell more of this fly during spring. I think it's most effective when fished down and across. While it's swinging, I like to give it a strip or two and let it fall back. It can also be worked through deeper holes and pockets in a jig fashion. That tactic works well on the Salmon River near Sunbeam."

Neon Prince Nymph

See photo of Prince Nymph	**Hook:** VMC 7062 or Daiichi 1280, sizes 10–18
	Thread: Black or brown 8/0 Cascade Supreme
	Body: Peacock herl
	Hackle: Soft hen hackle, brown
	Tail: Brown goose biots

Thorax: Peacock herl

Wing: White goose biots extending to the end of the body

Weight: .015 lead wire on sizes 12–18

Wing Case: Four strands of pearlescent Cascade Fly Flash or Flashabou

Rib: Pearlescent Crystal Hair or two strands of fine Flashabou twisted together

THE NEON PRINCE NYMPH IS A WARREN SCHOTH modification of the popular and infinitely productive standard Prince Nymph. Schoth's pattern basically adds more flash to the nymph, which attracts a trout's attention no matter where the pattern is fished.

"In my mind, more flash is better," Schoth said. "This is just a good all-around nymph that can be fished during a variety of hatches or just used as an attractor. When fished in a jerky motion, it serves as a caddis pupa emerger. If tied in small sizes and swam through the water, it's a good mayfly nymph pattern. If fished in a lake or reservoir, it may be taken for a shrimp. This pattern works extremely well at Magic Reservoir and Henry's Lake, plus the section of the Henry's Fork below Osborn Bridge."

No-Hackle (mayfly)

Hook: TMC 900BL, sizes 16, 18

Thread: Yellow

Wing: Gray duck quill

Tail: Blue dun hackle fibers

Body: Light yellow or olive Superfine Dubbing

ORIGINALLY INTRODUCED BY DOUG SWISHER and Carl Richards, the No-Hackle is one of the most productive spring-creek patterns in the world. Today the fly is associated with Mike Lawson and René Harrop, who tie splendid examples, but it doesn't get the notoriety or use it deserves. And, I must admit, I'm one of those anglers who has not given this pattern its due. But how could I—the No-Hackle is not durable, and once the wings split it's no good. Right?

"Everyone has misconceptions about this fly," said Mike Lawson, who has created numerous variations of the original. "People say it is not durable because the duck-quill wing doesn't hold together. People come into my shop to fish the Ranch section of the Henry's Fork and they don't want No-Hackles. They say it's a one-fish fly. I tell them I wouldn't ever fish the Ranch without some No-Hackles.

"The thing is, this pattern is most effective when the wing splits up, but that's when people think the fly is shot. Frankly, sometimes I'll take a brand-new No-Hackle and flare the wings out and break them up. You don't want to throw away a No-Hackle until the hook breaks, or it unravels, or you lose it to a fish.

"The main thing is to avoid tying the wings so they look perfect," Lawson urged. "Just tie it to look right. If the hackles split, big deal—you've saved yourself an extra step. I have to cast my flies several times to make them look that way."

The color combinations can be changed to represent many mayflies, including *Baetis, Callibaetis,* and Mahogany Duns.

North Fork Fly (attractor)

Hook:	Mustad 7957B, sizes 12–16
Thread:	Black monocord
Tail:	Goose quill dyed red or yellow
Body:	Peacock herl
Wing:	White calf tail
Hackle:	Brown

ANOTHER OF STAN YAMAMURA'S WONDERFUL creations, the North Fork Fly is one of eastern Idaho's most popular and productive attractor patterns.

Yamamura developed the fly specifically for the Henry's Fork, but it takes fish on all broken-water sections of fast-moving rivers. Its white calf tail wing shows like a beacon, making it an excellent choice for mountain streams. This fly is a reasonable substitute for the Royal Wulff, which is more difficult to tie.

Northern Pike Fly (streamer)

Hook:	Size 3/0 saltwater
Thread:	Fluorescent red
Head and Body:	White or tan rabbit strip
Tail:	White and red saddle hackle

THIS POPULAR PATTERN WAS HIGHLIGHTED in the book, *Flies of the Northwest*, and that was for good reason—the Northern Pike Fly catches those big toothy creatures wherever it is thrown. It is also an appealing fly because tyers can vary color schemes simply by changing the saddle hackle tail or the rabbit-strip body. In Idaho, the northern Panhandle holds the best pike options, which include the chain lakes and Lake Coeur d' Alene.

October Caddis Larva (nymph)

Hook: Mustad 37160, sizes 8–12

Tail: Dark Hungarian partridge

Rib: Fine copper wire

Thorax: Blend of brown rabbit, squirrel, and seal

Body: Blend of fibers from a golden Zonker strip, yellow seal, and golden retriever underfur

Head: Brass bead

Legs: Brown Hungarian partridge hackle fibers

THIS IS ANOTHER FAVORITE NORTHERN IDAHO pattern from Dan Curtis. According to Curtis, anglers should not limit their use of this nymph to the fall months.

"For some unknown reason, the October Caddis Larva abandons its protective shell of rocks and sticks and migrates to fast water in mid-June," Curtis said. "At that time there will be thousands of unprotected larvae drifting along the bottom of northern Idaho's rivers, and the trout gorge on them. The action lasts about two or three weeks, until they can build another case. They emerge again in October and are once again vulnerable to trout."

Otter Nymph

Hook: Mustad 3906, sizes 8–16

Tail: Brown partridge

Ribbing (optional): Fine copper wire

Body: Mixed otter and seal fur (picked)

Hackle: Brown partridge

See color photo

ONE OF THE "BUGGIEST" NYMPHS EVER CREATED, the Otter Nymph remains popular though you won't find it in too many fly bins today. This 1950s pattern is best tied on your own vise.

The fly's originator, Ted Trueblood, was one of the nation's greatest outdoor voices in the middle part of the twentieth century. He fished southwestern Idaho's waters religiously, and was able to take advantage of his job—he wrote for all the top outdoor magazines—to travel abroad.

Tied with a body of mixed otter and seal fur and a brown partridge hackle, this pattern represents nothing in particular and just about everything in general. It passes as a scud imitation, is a fine representation of caddis, and in a pinch it can be fished as a mayfly nymph.

Parachute Adams (mayfly)

Hook: TMC 900BL, sizes 10–20	
Thread: Gray	
Wing: Post of white calf tail or poly yarn	
Tail: Grizzly hackle fibers	
Body: Gray Antron or Superfine Dubbing	

Hackle: Grizzly

Note: This is a regular Adams with a parachute hackle.

THE PARACHUTE ADAMS, which matches the duns of many mayfly species, is one of the West's most popular patterns, and its status is no less impressive in Idaho.

The Parachute Adams' popularity stems from its calf tail or poly yarn post. The post is highly visible at a distance, even in choppy water. And the parachute hackle wound around the post allows the fly to sit low in the surface film, which presents trout with an appealing silhouette. Because of these traits, the Parachute Adams works well in a variety of waters, including roily freestone streams and tailwaters, and even flat-water spring creeks and lowland still waters. It's also a great pattern on high-mountain lakes.

Parachute Ant (terrestrial)

Hook: TMC 900, sizes 14–20

Thread: Black

Wing: White calf body hair

Abdomen: Black Antron

Hackle: Grizzly

Head: Black Antron

There are many productive ant patterns, but I've found none more effective than the Parachute Ant, which was created by Ed Schroeder.

Fished on freestone streams, tailwater rivers, or delicate spring creeks, the Parachute Ant rides the surface nicely, and its calf body hair wing is highly visible. When fishing small ant patterns during late summer and fall, a visible wing is a godsend.

This pattern is most effective when fished close to grassy banks, or along banks with overhanging trees or vegetation. However, it will also take fish from the middle of the stream. This ant pattern is a great choice if you have risen and missed a fish on a hopper pattern and it refuses to rise to that large terrestrial again. For some reason, in those situations, trout seem to respond to an ant.

Pheasant Tail Twist Nymph

Hook: Standard nymph, sizes 16–24

Thread: Brown

Tail: Two pheasant tail fibers

Body: Pheasant tail fiber and orange Antron touch dubbing (twisted together in a dubbing loop)

Wing Case: Six pheasant tail fibers

Abdomen: Olive Antron (touch dubbed)

In small sizes, 18 through 24, this bright nymph matches the *Baetis* nymph. Even when not match anything in particular, it is effective on spring creeks and tailwaters. The brightness of this Gary LaFontaine fly is provided by Antron, trilobal nylon.

Philo Betto (streamer)

See color photo	
	Hook: Mustad 9672, sizes 4–8
	Thread: Olive or black
	Tail: Pheasant rump dyed olive, and with the underfeather removed. Add ten or twelve strands of silver Krystal Flash
Body: Palmered, olive-dyed pheasant rump	

PHILO BETTO WAS THE NAME OF CLINT EASTWOOD's character in the movie *Every Which Way But Loose*. But today in Idaho, that name is more often associated with the excellent streamer pattern created by Scott Schnebly, who owns Lost River Outfitters in Ketchum.

"It's a bad-ass fly, so we named it after a bad-ass character," Schnebly said. "The Philo Betto represents a sculpin, and it will fish well in every water you throw it in as long as its color matches the bottom of the stream. All baitfish seem to acquire a camouflage that matches the strata they live in, so it pays to tie streamer patterns that match that color. Olive is the most effective color for the Philo, but gray is good, too."

Although most streamers are made more effective by adding weight directly to the hook, Schnebly warns anglers not to add lead to the Philo's body.

"It doesn't work as well if lead is tied to the hook," Schnebly said. "Doing that destroys the action of the filoplume. Instead of tying lead to the hook, I prefer to fish it with a split shot attached 12 to 14 inches above the fly. That allows the filoplume to keep its action and the fly remains just above bottom. You can also tie in a beadhead or a conehead, but I think it undulates best without that weight."

Schnebly typically fishes the Philo Betto quartering

downstream. "As it swings across the current, I pull on the line with my left hand to make it dart, then I let it slide back into the current. When it hits your side of the river, strip it back in 4-inch strips, which mimics the movements of an actual sculpin.

"I first fished this pattern on the Big Wood, and I caught seven fish between 15 and 19 inches on a piece of water I'd just taken a guide-trip through. I've also caught steelhead and bass on the fly. It works well in lakes, but it's best when fished on a stream."

Prince Nymph

Hook: TMC 5263, sizes 6–16

Thread: Black

Tail: Brown goose or turkey biots

Rib: Flat gold tinsel

Body: Peacock

Legs: Brown or furnace hackle

Wing: White goose or turkey biots

Head (optional): Copper bead

THE PRINCE NYMPH ORIGINATED IN CALIFORNIA in the 1940s, and it didn't take long to establish itself as one of the "Big Three" nymphs of the northern Rocky Mountain region (the Hare's Ear, the Pheasant Tail, and the Prince are likely the three most popular nymphs in Idaho). It's also rated as one of the top sellers in every fly shop in the state.

Fish the Prince Nymph in sizes 6 to 16 on any of Idaho's freestone streams, tailwater rivers, spring creeks, or still waters. Because they are most effective when dead-drifted along the bottom rocks or swung across holding areas, beadhead Prince Nymphs generally outfish unweighted versions. When there are no hatches occurring and you must go beneath the surface, the Prince Nymph is a prime choice.

Quigley Cripple (mayfly)

Hook:	TMC 900BL, sizes 14–18
Thread:	Tan
Shuck:	Brown or tan Z-Lon over brown marabou
Body:	Pheasant tail fibers
Rib:	Fine copper wire
Thorax:	Yellow poly yarn or Superfine Dubbing
Wing:	Deer hair
Hackle:	Grizzly

I WASN'T IMPRESSED WHEN I FIRST laid eyes on this fly. It is a chaotic combination of fur, hair, marabou feathers, and dubbing; it more resembles a drowned swallow than a dainty mayfly imitation. How, I asked, could a fly like that possibly fool a fish in heavy, broken current, let alone draw a fish to the top on a slick-surfaced spring creek?

Obviously, the fly's inventor had tipped too many martinis before he'd sat down at the vice. That fly, I declared, was a strong case against the bottle.

As they say, looks can be deceiving.

The fly in question was a PMD emerger pattern called the Quigley Cripple. It was tied on a size-16 hook.

Today, the Quigley Cripple, created by Bob Quigley, is usually the first fly I try when I encounter mayflies, whether on a large river, a lake, or even a delicate spring creek. Trout eat them like candy.

Gary LaFontaine believes that the Quigley Cripple is so effective because it matches an emergent stage, when insects are most vulnerable to trout.

"It's just a fact that at some point a trout will eat emergers that are half in, half out of, the water," he said. "Those are the easiest flies to catch and the cripple is an excellent rough emerger pattern. You can catch trout on that pattern during an entire mayfly hatch, but I think the major time for cripples is late in the hatch when crippled and stillborn mayflies collect in the surface film in backwaters and eddies. That's when you'll see some real torpedoes sucking them out of the scum."

Rabbit-Strip Leech (streamer)

Hook: TMC, sizes 2–6

Thread: Black

Body: Black, olive or brown rabbit

I TIE THIS PATTERNS WHEN ONLY A FEW min-utes remain before a fishing partner arrives and I need a big fly, a baitfish, or a leech imitation that offers plenty of movement. To tie this pattern all you have to do is attach the rabbit strip to the hook shank, just above the bend, then simply wind the rabbit forward and tie off near the eye, leaving enough room to design a thread head. This pattern, as evidenced by my rendition in the photo, does not need to be pretty. An ugly pattern will catch just as many fish, maybe even more, than one that you can sell to a fly shop. I've used Rabbit-Strip Leeches on Idaho's South Fork Boise, Silver Creek, and South Fork Snake rivers with good success. They are also very effective in Montana, especially, I've found, on the Bighorn River during winter. They will likely work wherever you try them, especially on waters that harbor big, fish-eating brown trout.

Renegade (attractor)

Hook: TMC 100, sizes 8–16

Thread: Black

Rib: Gold wire

Tag: Gold Mylar

Rear Hackle: Brown

Body: Peacock herl

Front Hackle: White

See color photo

CREATED IN THE 1930S by Taylor "Beartracks" Williams, who lived in Ketchum, Idaho, the Renegade is a standard for high-mountain lake and mountain stream fly fishers across the West.

Tied with Fore and Aft–style hackles and a body of peacock herl, the Renegade matches no insect in particular, but it's certainly "buggy" and fish destroy it. This fly can be fished either dry or wet.

Although the Renegade is not suited to demanding spring creeks or flat sections of tailwaters, it excels on mountain freestone streams such as the Big Wood River, the Payette River, Kelly Creek, the North Fork Clearwater, the Lochsa, the Selway, and the St. Joe Rivers. Cutthroat trout are typically less wary than either rainbows or browns, and they most often mistake the Renegade for an ant or beetle. Because of its excellent visibility, the Renegade is a great choice for choppy, boulder-strewn pocket water.

Royal Trude (attractor)

See color photo of the Trude	**Hook:** TMC 5212, sizes 6–18
	Thread: Black
	Body: Peacock herl and red floss
	Tail: Deer or red hackle fibers
	Wing: White calf tail
Hackle: Brown	

A VARIATION OF CARTER HARRISON'S standard Trude, the Royal Trude offers all the qualities of the Trude with the white calf wing that gives increased visibility. The Royal Trude is an excellent attractor dry-fly choice when fishing roily current where visibility is key.

Royal Wulff (attractor)

Hook: TMC 100, sizes 10–22

Thread: Black

Wing: White calf tail

Tail: Elk hair, moose hair, brown bucktail or calf tail

Rib: Fine gold wire

Body: Peacock and red floss

Hackle: Brown

THERE ARE FEW FLY SHOPS IN THIS COUNTRY that don't stock a healthy supply of the Royal Wulff, perhaps the most popular attractor pattern in Idaho. The Wulff style was created by legendary fly fisher Lee Wulff in the late 1920s. The Royal Wulff, one of many color variations, has been tested on every water type imaginable—and it produces.

Typically tied in sizes 10 through 16, the Royal Wulff is best fished in roily water, where its flotation and visibility are superb. A prime choice on northern Idaho's cutthroat streams, it is an excellent pattern when fishing tributaries of major rivers, such as the Falls River (Henry's Fork), Trail Creek (Big Wood River), Kelly Creek (Clearwater), and Loon Creek (Middle Fork Salmon).

When tied size 20 or smaller, the Royal Wulff is also an effective spring, fall, and winter pattern. Whether fish take it for a midge is difficult to say—but in any case, they eat it.

The only disadvantage to the Royal Wulff is the time required to tie it. With its body of peacock herl and red floss, divided calf tail wing, and heavy hackle, this fly requires patience at the vise.

Sadie Thompson Woolly Bugger (streamer)

Hook: 3X-long, size 8

Thread: Black or red

Body: Cherry pearl Crystal Chenille

Tail: Red marabou and pearl Krystal Flash

Hackle: Red saddle hackle

See color
photo

Clayne Baker, who ran Stonefly Anglers for many years and remains a resident of Boise, created the Sadie Thompson Woolly Bugger in the mid-1990s. The streamer, which was named after a long-legged prostitute in one of Baker's favorite novels (inspiration arrives in all forms), is a killer on southern Idaho's desert-country reservoirs, such as Sheep Creek, Mormon, Little Camas, and Magic.

"That fly has really caught on and a lot of guys in this area are asking for it," Baker said. "It's tied with cherry-colored Crystal Chenille with a red marabou tail, just like that prostitute's dress. It's really hot on the desert reservoirs and it's been pretty effective on Henry's Lake, too. It works anytime, but spring and fall, for some reason, seem to be the best times to fish the Sadie Thompson."

Sculpin Minnow (streamer)

Hook: Mustad 79580, sizes 2–6	
Rib: Gold tinsel	
Body: Brown, olive, or yellow polypropylene yarn	
Fins: Blue Hungarian partridge feather	
Tail and Dorsal Fin: Two cree saddle hackles	

Head: Deer hair, spun and clipped

Weight: Lead wrapped around hook shank

This is one of the most attractive and effective sculpin imitations you'll find in Idaho. Created by Dan Curtis, the Sculpin Minnow is a trophy trout-getter wherever large brown trout are found.

According to biologists, when trout measure 20 inches or more, insects make up only a small part of their diet. Baitfish, and especially sculpins, are the main forage of big fish in Idaho's freestone and tailwater streams. For this reason, the Sculpin Minnow is an excellent choice when fishing for giant browns on such waters as the lower Henry's Fork, the South Fork Snake, Silver Creek, the

Little Wood, the lower Big Wood, the Snake, the Portneuf, and Willow Creek.

This pattern is most effective when fished among the bottom rocks, so the hook shank should be wrapped generously with lead wire beneath the yarn body. Sink-tip lines also help the fly reach bottom. Retrieve the fly in short, quick strips with occasional pauses. The Sculpin Minnow also takes fish when it swings across the current.

Serendipity

Hook: TMC 2487, sizes 8–22

Thread: Red, black, brown, or olive, to match the color of the natural

Rib: Fine gold or silver wire

Abdomen: Antron yarn or Z-Lon

Head: Spun deer hair, clipped to shape

MIDGES ARE PRESENT, IN ASTOUNDING numbers, in all of Idaho's trout waters. The Serendipity, popularized on Montana's Madison River by Ross Merigold, is an effective midge pattern that can be fished in the surface film or fully sunk. In the surface film, the pattern's deer-hair head keeps the fly afloat, and it is taken by trout as an emerging midge. Fished under a split shot or behind a beadhead nymph, such as the Prince Nymph or the Hare's Ear, the Serendipity is a solid midge-pupa pattern. Whether you're fishing a lake or stream, the Serendipity should draw strikes.

Sheep Creek Special (nymph)

Hook: Mustad 9672, sizes 6–16

Thread: Olive

Body: Olive chenille

Hackle: Brown

Wing: Mallard breast feather

See color
photo

IF YOU ARE PURSUING LARGE TROUT in an Idaho lake or
reservoir, bring several Sheep Creek Specials. Created in the
early 1960s by George Biggs of Jerome, Idaho, this pattern
really takes still-water trout. Biggs initially discovered the
fly's merit while fishing it on southern Idaho's Sheep Creek
Reservoir, but the pattern produced well on other reservoirs,
including Montana's Clark Canyon Reservoir, where it has
become a standard.

The Sheep Creek Special is particularly effective in
waters containing dense *Callibaetis* mayfly and damselfly
populations. During *Callibaetis* hatches, the fly is a suitable
emerger imitation. Fished as a damsel nymph, trout crush
this pattern when it is stripped slowly over submerged vegetation. Although the Sheep Creek Special can be fished near
the surface, it is most often worked with a sinking line.

Short Wing Emerger (mayfly)

Hook: TMC 100, sizes 16–18	
Tail: Wood duck	
Rib: Fine copper wire	
Wing: Mallard wing quill segment	
Body: Pink Cahill dubbing blend	

Legs: Hungarian partridge

CREATED IN THE EARLY 1970S by René Harrop, the Short
Wing Emerger has been tested thoroughly on Idaho's waters,
and it continues to produce admirably today.

Fly fishers on the South Fork Boise River should pay particular attention to this fly, which is intended to match
Epeorus albertae or the Pink Albert (also known as the Pink
Cahill or Pink Lady). During July and August, the South
Fork Boise hosts one of the state's best *Epeorus albertae*
emergences. Fortunately for the fly fisher, it comes off during
the heat of the day when there are no other hatches.

The Short Wing Emerger is designed to mimic the Pink

Albert's unique emergence tactic. Unlike most mayflies, the Pink Albert sheds its nymphal shuck near the bottom of the stream, then rises to the surface as a fully formed adult. Trout key in on this emerger pattern because its wings are easy to see.

When fishing the South Fork Boise, my friends fish a Pink Albert dun pattern (a sparkle dun works well) on the surface. To the eye or bend of the hook they attach a 14-inch section of 5X or 6X tippet material and tie the Short Wing Emerger to the end of it. They cover rises with the dun and use it as a strike indicator for the emerger. When fishing this rig, watch the point fly (that is, the dun) carefully. If it pauses or twitches, or if you see a swirl just behind it, set the hook.

"The Short Wing Emerger can be fished alone," Harrop said, "but it probably works best when fished in tandem with a dun. I think that's the way to go when fishing this pattern."

Shroud (mayfly)

Hook: 3X fine wire, sizes 8–10

Tail: Red Marabou fibers

Body: Gray mink fur dubbed, with guard hairs in a very bristly body about halfway up the hook shank

Hackle: Blue dun (three feathers with the dull side forward, covering the forward half of the shank)

THIS IS A HOT FLY LATELY ON IDAHO LAKES during *Callibaetis* time. Twitch it and the slithering marabou tail just about guarantees that cruising trout will come to the fly. It is a dry-fly Woolly Bugger. Don't worry about the marabou sinking this fly. It won't. Put floatant on the hackle and body and the marabou will hang just under the surface on this Gary LaFontaine pattern.

In size 10 the Shroud will match the Gray Drake hatch on Idaho rivers, especially the Henry's Fork, and in sizes 8 to 16 it will imitate the *Callibaetis*.

Slow Water Caddis

See color photo	**Hook:** TMC 900BL, sizes 12–16
	Thread: Gray
	Body: Olive Antron or Superfine Dubbing
	Hackle: Blue dun clipped underneath
	Underwing: Gray deer or elk tied downwing-style

Overwing: Quill wing or blue dun hen saddle coated with Dave's Flexament

Antennae: Gray hackle stems

If you're looking for a perfect caddisfly imitation, look no further. René Harrop's Slow Water Caddis is as realistic as they come. For that reason, it's an excellent choice when fishing still waters and flat sections of spring creeks, tailwaters, and freestone streams, where trout have plenty of time to inspect an offering.

"The realistic image is a huge advantage when you are fishing ultra-clear water conditions where the trout are super-selective," said Harrop, who uses this fly often on the Henry's Fork. "It rides real low in the water [due to its clipped hackle] like a spent caddis, but it has a little more realistic look."

Sparkle Dun (mayfly)

Hook: TMC 900BL, sizes 14–20
Thread: Yellow
Wing: Deer hair
Shuck: Brown Z-Lon
Body: Yellow Antron or Superfine Dubbing

Note: This dressing is for the Pale Morning Dun, but by changing the color of the body, shuck, and thread, it can be dressed to match any species of mayfly.

This pattern was adapted from the famous Caucci and Nastasi ComparaDun. Created in the mid-1980s by Craig Mathews and John Juracek of Blue Ribbon Flies in West Yellowstone, the Sparkle Dun is one of Idaho's most widely used patterns. With its highly visible trailing shuck, the Sparkle Dun matches stillborn and injured mayflies, which appear in vast numbers during emergences. Trout key in on those unfortunate creatures and swallow them by the truckload. The Sparkle Dun, which is very easy to tie and requires no hackle, is easy to see on flat-surfaced spring creeks and lakes. It is also visible in a moderate chop, which makes it a perfect choice on a variety of waters.

Spent CDC Caddis

Hook: TMC 100, sizes 12–16

Thread: Olive

Abdomen: Fine olive dubbing

Underwing: Elk hair

Overwing: Paired wild mallard CDC feathers, medium dun

Thorax: Brown dubbing

Legs: Pull the butts of the CDC feathers along the side of the fly and trim them to half the length of the body

"To MATCH CADDIS, THIS IS PROBABLY my favorite fly in terms of how often I use it," said René Harrop, who runs the House of Harrop in St. Anthony. "It has a low profile and it's very effective in the evening, especially on spring creeks and tailwaters. It floats well, but you can doctor it up a little to make it fish like an emerger, if needed."

Spent Partridge Caddis

Hook: TMC 100, sizes 12–16

Thread: Olive or tan

Body: Olive or tan Superfine Dubbing

Wing: Dark brown mottled partridge feathers, tied spent-wing style

Hackle: Grizzly and brown

Thorax: Peacock herl

See color photo

THIS PATTERN ORIGINATED WHEN MIKE LAWSON became frustrated with hen hackle and its inability to hold its shape when wet.

"I realized that the wild birds, like quail, grouse, and especially [Hungarian] partridge, really hold their shape," Lawson said. "When wet, a hen hackle slims down and it's tough to see, but a partridge feather, even on the small patterns, is pretty easy to see."

The Spent Partridge Caddis is most effective when adult female caddis return to a river to lay their eggs. This usually occurs during the last hour of light, but is not always the case: Several species lay their eggs in the morning. You can usually tell if caddis are laying eggs simply by their presence on the water.

"If you see caddis drifting on the water for a long way, they are probably laying eggs," Lawson said. "Caddis do not tend to spend a lot of time on the water unless they are doing that. If you see that situation, tie on the Spent Partridge Caddis—it's one of my favorite patterns."

St. Joe Special and St. Joe Favorite (caddisflies)

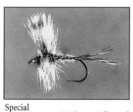

Special

Hook: Mustad 94840, sizes 10–18	
Tail: Grizzly hackle fiber tips (golden pheasant tips on the St. Joe favorite)	
Body: Gray dubbing	
Hackle: Grizzly	
Wing: Blue dun or gray turkey flat	

THESE PATTERNS, WHICH VARY ONLY in color and tail construction, originated in northern Idaho's native westslope cutthroat country, and they were tested extensively on the St. Joe and North Fork Clearwater Rivers. Anglers continue to include these patterns in their arsenal, and they are stocked in all of northern Idaho's fly shops—a true indication of their effectiveness.

The St. Joe Special was originally tied to imitate caddis-flies, which it does adequately, but it is a dead ringer for a large mayfly, such as early season March Brown Drakes. Tied in the appropriate colors and sizes, the St. Joe also matches Green and Brown Drakes.

"I believe originally it was intended to match the October caddis that we see on the St. Joe," said Dan Curtis, a busy fly tyer who lives in Coeur d'Alene. "I don't know why they made it look so much like a mayfly, but it sure is an effective match."

Because of its heavy hackle and tall wing, the St. Joe rides high, and is especially effective on the rocky cutthroat waters of northern Idaho. However, it will take fish during mayfly hatches and spinner falls on every freestone and tailwater stream in the state.

Stan's Hopper (terrestrial)

Hook: Mustad 9672, sizes 4–8

Thread: Black monocord

Underbody: Yellow chenille

Overbody and Tail: Bunched deer hair, with tips forming the tail

Wings: Turkey quill segments

Hackle: Two grizzly and one brown saddle hackle

STAN YAMAMURA PRODUCED THIS HOPPER in an effort to improve upon the flotation of the Joe's Hopper and to create a fly that could be tied a little easier. Stan's Hopper offers added buoyancy via extra deer hair tied to the body of the fly. Turkey quill segments are attached in front of the body and the fly is finished with a collar of two grizzly saddle hackles and one brown saddle hackle. Due to its extra hair and abundant hackle, this fly rides high and is an excellent choice in choppy water. It's also an adequate match for giant stoneflies.

Stan's Willow Fly (stonefly)

See color photo	
Hook: Mustad 7957B, sizes 14–16	
Thread: Monocord	
Body: Yellow thread	
Wing: Light elk hair	
Hackle: Grizzly and brown	

IF YOU ARE LOOKING FOR AN EASILY TIED FLY that matches caddis and the small stonefly species that are abundant on Idaho's freestone and tailwater streams, Stan's Willow Fly is a tough pattern to beat.

Stan's Willow Fly was created in the 1960s by Stan Yamamura to match the Yellow Sally, a size-14 stonefly that hatches profusely in riffles and really brings trout to the top. Other anglers soon found that it also matched various caddis species, and it quickly supplanted established caddis patterns.

Stayner's Ducktail (nymph/wet fly)

See color photo	
Hook: Mustad 9672, sizes 4–8	
Thread: Olive or black	
Tail: Orange hackle	
Body: Olive chenille	
Rib: Flat gold tinsel	

Wing: Mallard breast feather

Hackle: Orange

IF FORCED TO FISH ONLY ONE PATTERN for the rest of their lives, many of Idaho's long-time fly fishers would choose Stayner's Ducktail. Ruel Stayner, who lived in Twin Falls and created the Ducktail in the 1960s, found the pattern productive on local waters such as Richfield Canal, the lower Big Wood River, Magic Reservoir, and the Little Wood River. The Ducktail is particularly effective on still waters. It is also called Ruel's Ducktail.

Stimulator (caddisfly/stonefly)

Hook: TMC 200R, sizes 4–14

Thread: Fluorescent orange

Tail: Elk hair

Rib: Fine gold or copper wire

Abdomen: Fluorescent yellow Antron palmered with ginger hackle

Wing: Flared elk hair

Hackle: Grizzly

Thorax: Amber Antron

THIS IS ONE OF THE MOST POPULAR PATTERNS in the West and is a mainstay in Idaho as well. Randall Kaufmann, who runs Kaufmann's Streamborn in Portland, Oregon, created this fly, which is an adequate match for a variety of insects.

Dressed with yellow Antron, the Stimulator matches the Yellow Sally and other golden stoneflies. With a black body, the Stimulator takes fish during salmon fly emergences. Tied in tan, olive, or orange, the Stimulator matches many caddis species, including the large October caddis, which is present on many of Idaho's freestone and tailwater streams.

Because of its heavy dressing, the Stimulator rides high, and is very effective in broken water and heavy riffles.

Super Renegade (wet fly)

Hook: Mustad 9672 or 79580, sizes 4–10

Thread: Black monocord

Tip (optional): Gold Mylar

Rear Hackle: Grizzly or brown saddle

Rear Body: Black, olive, brown, yellow, or white chenille

Middle Hackle: Grizzly or brown saddle

Front Body: Peacock herl; or black, olive, brown, yellow, or white chenille

Front Hackle: White saddle

Perhaps no other fly is as indelibly tied to Idaho as the Super Renegade. Created by Ardell Jeppsen of Labell, Idaho, as he fought the effects of polio in an area hospital, the Super Renegade is a fixture in the fly boxes of those who fish the South Fork Snake. Initially called the Hooligan, the Super Renegade is particularly effective on the South Fork Snake due to that river's abundance of large stoneflies.

Whether fished in high water or during the lower flows of fall, the Super Renegade draws trout from under logjams, sweepers, undercut banks, and overhanging brush. The Super Renegade is tied in a variety of color schemes.

Swannundaze Chironomid (midge nymph)

Hook: TMC 200R, sizes 16–20	
Thread: Olive, red, brown, or black	
Abdomen: Olive, red, brown, or black Swannundaze	
Thorax: Peacock herl	

Gills: White poly yarn

Boyd Aigner of Seattle developed this effective pattern in the lake region of western Washington. Today, the Swannundaze Chironomid is used on many of Idaho's still waters. It also takes fish on Idaho's rivers, especially during the winter.

When used in a lake or reservoir, the Swannundaze Chironomid can be fished with a sink-tip or full-sinking line to represent midge pupa. On a stream, it can be fished with a floating line under a strike indicator. Dead-drift it through slow-moving or slack water and keep an eye on the indicator. When the indicator pauses or leaps, set the hook.

Taylor Shrimp (nymph/scud)

Hook: Mustad 3906, standard shank, sizes 8–14	
Thread: Light olive	See color photo
Body: Gold and dark olive variegated chenille, size 00	
Hackle: Rip-dyed golden olive grizzly hackle fastened at the butt halfway down the bend of the shank	
Tail: Hackle tip	

CREATED BY MARV TAYLOR, the Taylor Shrimp is suggestive of large scuds, which are found in many of Idaho's large lakes and reservoirs.

"It's difficult to tie this pattern in the small sizes because they don't make chenille small enough," Taylor said, "but it's the best when tied to match larger scuds. It's particularly effective at Henry's Lake in sizes 8 through 14."

Among the very best of scud patterns, the Taylor Shrimp does double duty as a snail imitation.

"I tie them heavily weighted so they sink," Taylor said. "I find that I get a lot of takes as it drops down and settles near the bottom. I am absolutely sure fish are taking it at that time for a snail. If I don't get a strike while it's sinking, I go ahead and use a standard scud retrieve."

Teton Queen and Teton King (wet flies)

Queen Hook: Mustad 3399, sizes 8–16	
King Hook: Mustad 94840, sizes 8–16	
Thread: Black	
Body: Black silk	
Queen Hackle: Grizzly	
King Hackle: Furnace	Teton King

THE TETON QUEEN AND TETON KING were originally tied by Hazel Hansen at the N5 Ranch, located north of Tetonia. Their popularity spread across Idaho and neighboring states. Hansen supplied the patterns to Glen Evans in Caldwell,

Idaho, and Bob Carmichael in Jackson, Wyoming. They don't look like much when pinched in the jaws of a vise, but these flies are trout-getters. These patterns are easy to tie, and they are effective on all water types, from raging freestones to delicate spring creeks.

Fish these flies upstream and allow them to drift past you. Trout typically hammer them as they swing toward the surface, an action that imitates emerging insects. Anytime you encounter an emergence and do not have a specific imitation to match, tie on a Teton Queen or King and you will likely draw strikes.

Thorax PMD (mayfly)

Hook: TMC 100, sizes 16–18	
Thread: Pale olive	
Wing: Medium gray turkey flat	
Tail: Light dun hackle fibers	
Body: Pale yellow olive Antron	

Hackle: Light dun wound through wing

Note: Dressing is for the Pale Morning Dun

THORAX MAYFLY PATTERNS ARE EXCELLENT on flat-water sections of spring creeks, tailwaters, and freestone streams. They also fool selective still-water trout.

This pattern was tied by Mike Lawson, who adapted it from Vince Marinaro's original efforts. It offers a strong silhouette of the mayfly wing, which is especially important when trout key in on duns.

"When trout are feeding on duns, the first thing they see in their window of vision is an upright wing," Lawson said. "For this pattern I use a turkey flat wing and a good hackle, palmered over the dubbing to the head of the hook. Then I clip the hackle on the bottom.

"You have to be careful when clipping the hackle," Lawson added. "You don't want to clip it flat. Just clip it under the hook so it looks like a V with longer hackle coming down either side of the hook. Tied and clipped like that, this pattern is real effective for slow water and lake fishing, when those fish are cruising and sipping off the surface."

This fly can be tied to imitate *Baetis, Callibaetis,* Mahogany Duns, and Tricos.

TLF Midge (nymph/pupa)

Hook: Dai-Riki scud hook, sizes 16–20

Body: Red, black, purple, tan, or olive thread to match natural

Tail: Pheasant tail fibers cut short

Thorax: Seal and rabbit blended to match natural

Head: Glass bead to match natural

FIRST AND FOREMOST A MIDGE PATTERN, the TLF can also be dressed to match numerous small mayfly nymphs, including Pale Morning Duns and *Baetis.*

Dan Curtis, the fly's creator, developed the TLF to match "those tiny little expletives" he found clinging to his waders each time he fished the Beaverhead River.

"It's an excellent midge pattern," Curtis said, "that works on every water midges are found [virtually all waters]."

The TLF is an excellent choice for streams and still waters alike. It can be fished near the surface; however, it is most effective when it is dead-drifted near the bottom or allowed to swing from the bottom toward the surface.

Trico Poly-Wing Spinner (mayfly)

Hook: TMC 5230, sizes 20–24

Thread: Black

Wing: White poly yarn

Tail: Dark dun fibers, split

Abdomen: Stripped quill

Thorax: Black Superfine Dubbing

THIS PATTERN IS A MUST-HAVE DURING SUMMER Trico spinner falls. Although this pattern rides low on the water, its white poly wing makes it fairly visible, which is critical on flat-water spring creeks. I've found this to be one of the most productive patterns on south-central Idaho's Silver Creek.

This fly doubles as an excellent *Baetis* spinner imitation when tied with brown quill and brown Superfine. Selective trout often key in on *Baetis* spinners even when Trico spinners litter miles of the surface. Don't ask why—that's just trout for you. However, by having a few of these in your spring creek fly box, you'll have the *Baetis* spinner falls covered.

Trude (stonefly)

See color photo	**Hook:** Mustad 94840, sizes 4–8
	Thread: Black nylon
	Tail: Reddish brown hackle fibers
	Body: Red wool yarn
	Rib: Silver tinsel

Wing: Red fox squirrel tail

Hackle: Two reddish brown neck or saddle hackles

FEW ANGLERS KNOW THE STORY BEHIND the Trude's creation. It began as a joke by Carter Harrison in 1901 at Algenia Ranch near Island Park, Idaho. He tied the first one on an absurdly huge hook, but when subsequent smaller versions caught fish, the Trude and its wing style, known now as the Trude style, became popular in fly-fishing circles.

Today, there are hundreds, if not thousands, of patterns that are tied in the downwing Trude style. The original fly and its progeny work best to imitate stoneflies and large caddisflies. With a stiff neck or saddle hackle tied in front of the wing, the Trude-style fly is very buoyant and highly visible in broken current—again, good traits for a stonefly pattern.

Turck's Tarantula (attractor)

Hook: 3X-long dry fly, sizes 2–8

Body: Hare's mask dubbing

Tail: Amherst pheasant tail tippets

Legs: White, yellow, or black rubber

Wing: White calf tail and tan deer hair topped (optional) with pearl Krystal Flash

Head: Deer hair, spun and clipped

"HOW," YOU MAY ASK, "CAN A FLY THAT LARGE bring fish to the surface? It more resembles a drowned swallow than a trout fly."

I don't know the answer, but I assure you this fly will blow you away: It takes fish on every stream in the state.

The Turck's Tarantula was developed by Guy Turck in the cutthroat trout country surrounding Jackson, Wyoming. Its popularity quickly spread throughout the West after it was the winning fly in the Jackson Hole One-Fly Contest. Today, the Turck's Tarantula can be found in every fly bin in Idaho.

During late spring and early summer the Tarantula may suggest golden stoneflies or salmon flies, depending on the color of the body. During late summer and early fall, when grasshoppers are prime trout forage, an orange or yellow Tarantula draws fish to the top. This fly is extremely buoyant and is highly visible in riffled water. However, don't limit its use to tailwaters and freestone streams—the Turck's Tarantula takes large trout on demanding spring creeks and still waters as well.

Whiskey Creek (wet fly/nymph)

Hook: Mustad 7957B, sizes 6–12

Thread: Brown

Rear Hackle: White neck or saddle hackle

Body: Orange or brown thread

Front Hackle: Soft brown neck hackle

IN THE TRADITION OF FORE AND AFT–STYLE FLIES, the Whiskey Creek was created by O. S. Bybee of Soda Springs for use on the Bear and Blackfoot rivers. This pattern is effective when dead-drifted, or when allowed to swing across the current at the end of a drift to simulate an emerger. It's also an excellent alpine- and lowland-lake pattern.

Whitlock's Mouserat

Hook: TMC 8089, sizes 2–6	
Thread: White (back); black (front)	
Tail: Tan chamois	
Body: Deer hair	
Ears: Tan chamois	
Head: Clipped deer hair	
Whiskers: Black moose hair	

THE MOUSERAT, CREATED BY DAVE WHITLOCK, is a standard mouse pattern that takes bass and trout, plus pike, with regularity. Where mice patterns are sold, you usually find the Mouserat—it is not difficult to tie and it casts a nice silhouette. The Mouserat can be skittered across the surface of lakes or bounced off of lily pads and cattails. On a river it can be swung at the end of a drift or stripped across the surface.

X-Caddis

Hook: TMC 100, sizes 12–20	
Thread: Olive	
Body: Antron—olive, tan, black, or brown	
Shuck: Z-Lon	
Wing: Mottled deer hair	
Head: Clipped deer-hair butts	

DEVELOPED IN THE EARLY 1980s by Craig Mathews of West Yellowstone, Montana, the X-Caddis' reputation quickly moved south into Idaho, where it is an excellent choice during spring, summer, and fall caddis emergences. Effective on tailwater rivers, spring creeks, and freestone streams, the X-Caddis generally works best during summer evenings when caddisflies are caught in the surface film, struggling out of their nymphal shuck. This fly should be fished with a greased wing, which keeps part of the body above water.

Zonker (streamer)

Hook: TMC 300, sizes 2–6

Thread: White

Underbody: Wire bent to shape

Body: Copper Mylar (may use various colors)

Wing: Cream rabbit strip

Overwing: Pearl Accent Flash

Throat: Cream rabbit

Eyes: Yellow with black pupil

THIS FLY SHOULD BE LISTED IN THE JACK-OF-ALL-TRADES category; it is an excellent trout pattern, takes steelhead, terrorizes bass and, when tied in large sizes, it makes a decent pike fly.

When fishing warmwater species, the Zonker is especially effective when stripped across the surface. When allowed to dead-drift along the bottom rocks of deep river pools, it takes big brown trout, bull trout, and even minnow-seeking rainbows. It is also effective when strip-retrieved.

CHAPTER THREE
Fly Fishing Waters of Idaho

SMALL STREAMS

BECAUSE THEY SEE LESS FISHING PRESSURE than do Idaho's larger, big-name rivers, small streams offer a respite for fly fishers who covet solitude and eager fish.

In general, small streams produce small trout. But, when fishing a small stream, keep in mind that everything's relative. A 16-inch fish may not turn heads on the Henry's Fork, but taken from a tiny water, it's a trophy worthy of a streamside toast.

Some anglers may scoff at this notion, but isn't taking a fish under difficult circumstances the true appeal of our sport? The small-stream angler is often required to cast with pinpoint accuracy while being hemmed in by brush and surrounded by overhanging limbs and downed logs. Indeed, many fly fishers would argue that there is no greater challenge than the small stream.

For these reasons, Idaho's small streams remain popular destinations for those who adore them and worthwhile diversions for the angler seeking to avoid the chaos that is occasionally encountered on the major rivers (especially when the famous hatches come off).

Fortunately for Idaho's fly anglers, the Gem State offers thousands of miles of quality small-stream fishing. As you will find, attractor patterns and small nymphs come into their own on small streams, and usually will suffice. However, trout will be trout wherever you find them, so as a precautionary measure it pays to carry a variety of flies.

When fishing Idaho's small streams there are several important things you should keep in mind. First, remember that small streams fish wonderfully just after spring runoff, when you'll encounter excellent insect hatches and good

numbers of resident trout as well as larger migratory spawners. Mid- to late summer can prove challenging due to low,
clear water conditions. However, in some cases, this period
offers excellent opportunities for big trout that have moved
from the larger rivers into the tributaries seeking cooler
water. This is particularly true on northern Idaho's cutthroat
waters, including tributaries of the Selway, the Lochsa, the St.
Joe, and the Clearwater Rivers, as well as Kelly Creek.

Listed below are some of Idaho's best small-stream fisheries, along with a good selection of fly patterns appropriate
to those waters.

Bear Creek: This Palisades Reservoir tributary offers
spring-run cutthroat trout and fall-run browns. Fish this
stream during the prime time and you'll never forget it.

Birch Creek: An eastern Idaho rainbow trout bonanza.

Cayuse Creek: A Kelly Creek tributary that hosts spawn-
ing trout and midsummer main-stem refugees.

East Fork Big Lost River: Set in Copper Basin, one of
the most beautiful places in the West, the East Fork offers
brook trout and a few sizable rainbows. But whether or not
you catch any large fish, it's still a treat to fish. Keep an eye
out for a mid-June to mid-July Green Drake hatch.

Lemhi River: Located just east of Salmon, Idaho, the
Lemhi has been brutalized by man, but it still offers some
rainbow trout. However, the largest fish are found in the private stretches.

Loon Creek: To reach this Middle Fork Salmon River
tributary requires a long hike. However, by midsummer,
those who reach its seductive waters are treated to eager cutthroats and some large bull trout. A bonus for those reaching
this creek are the numerous hot springs that stretch along
much of its length.

Pahsimeroi River: Tucked away between the Lemhi and
Pahsimeroi ranges, this stream holds some large rainbow and
cutthroat trout—provided you can get permission to fish

from local landowners.

Pine Creek: A South Fork Snake River tributary that opens July 1st and offers some sizable cutthroat and rainbow spawners.

St. Mary's River (near Clarkia): This river clears earlier than the nearby St. Joe, which makes it a decent early-season bet for modest rainbows and cutthroats.

Stump, Willow, and Crow Creeks: These three streams twist out of the mountains east of Soda Springs. They host resident trout as well as large fall-run browns.

Trail Creek: Located just east of Sun Valley, this little stream offers eager rainbows and beaver ponds full of brook trout.

Upper South Fork Boise River: Not as popular as its tailwater section downstream, the upper South Fork offers rainbow, cutthroat, and even bull trout. These fish are not as large as their downstream cousins, but they're present in good numbers and they rise eagerly to dry-fly attractors.

Warm Springs Creek: Located west of Ketchum, this water produces sizable, wary rainbows throughout the season.

Flies for Idaho's Small Streams
    Bitch Creek Nymph
    CDC Rusty Spinner
    Elk Hair Caddis
    Gold-Ribbed Hare's Ear
    Light Variant
    Mackay Special
    Parachute Adams
    Parachute Ant
    Pheasant Tail Twist Nymph
    Prince Nymph
    Royal Wulff
    Trude
    Turck's Tarantula

High-Mountain Lakes

Some of the most foolish trout in the world live above 6,000 feet in Idaho's mountain lakes. However, even these fish prove quite picky at times, so it pays to take along a good selection of flies when heading to the high country. (Incidentally, there are no fly shops in the alpine country, so stock up before you strap on those hiking boots.)

Idaho is blessed with an array of mountain lakes. No matter where in the state you are, a quality mountain lake is close by. These waters can be unpredictable, however. Some lakes suffer heavy winter kill. If a lake makes it through the winter, you may find it populated with holdover trout exceeding 16 inches. Two friends and I fished a lake in the Sawtooth Mountains one fall and landed 84 cutthroat trout over 14 inches!

To reach that high-mountain lake—I'd be lynched if I revealed its name—required a 5-mile bike trip in, plus a 4-mile vertical bushwhack. However, upon exiting the mountains and reaching our vehicle after dark—absolutely exhausted—we declared the trip a wild success.

Mountain lakes are not easily accessed, and therefore offer the solitude that many fly fishers covet. As a rule, the farther a lake lies from the trailhead, the fewer the people who visit it. Because of their remoteness, most of Idaho's high-mountain lakes are best reached on horseback. If you're like me, however, and have no horse, you must do the entire trip on foot. This isn't a bad option, provided you don't mind carrying a 50- or 60-pound backpack.

Your backpack should be loaded with emergency food and water, plus a first-aid kit. Although you can fish most mountain lakes from shore, a float tube gives you unlimited access to the water. A float tube, waders, and fins add significant weight to your backpack, but the extra effort pays off with more fish brought to the net.

Because mountain weather is so unpredictable—even July and August may see freezing temperatures or snow storms—you must pack foul-weather gear with you. Lightening storms are common in the high country during summer. When a thunderhead approaches, it's critical that you get off the water and seek cover.

Despite the quirky nature of mountain weather, and despite the effort required to reach them, Idaho's mountain lakes are a treat to visit, and they offer some of the most spectacular scenery on the planet. Depending on the weather, I try to spend a week or more at a high-mountain lake each year from late-July through September. Give Idaho's mountain lakes a try and you won't be disappointed.

Below is a list of Idaho's prime mountain ranges, along with a selection of flies that work best on their alpine lakes:

Boulder/White Cloud Mountains: Located near Sun Valley, these lakes offer excellent angling opportunities. They, too, are connected by fine trail systems. Maps and lake information can be obtained at the Sawtooth National Recreation Area Headquarters (SNRA), located just north of Ketchum.

Copper Basin: The Pioneer Mountains surround this basin, and dozens of quality waters are within reach of the backpacking angler. Excellent trail systems connect these lakes, and most can be reached within a few hours.

Lemhi Range: Located just east of Salmon, the Lemhi's offer some excellent cutthroat trout lakes that see little pressure. Best accessed by horse, most of the Lemhi's lakes require overnight trips.

Sawtooth Mountains: The Sawtooths offer some of the best mountain-lake fishing in the world, and many provide the opportunity for excellent extended pack trips. Hundreds of lakes dot the Sawtooths, and you can get current information on their status by calling the Idaho Department of Fish and Game in Salmon, or by contacting the SNRA.

Seven Devils Mountains: Located in the Hell's Canyon

Wilderness Area, these lakes offer an excellent diversion from chukar hunting or rafting down the Snake River. These lakes are prime targets for those on horseback, but they're also within reach of backpackers. This is wonderful country, and an angler could easily spend a couple of weeks in the Seven Devils every year.

FLIES FOR IDAHO'S HIGH-MOUNTAIN LAKES

Brassie
Carey Special
CDC Biot ComparaDun *Callibaetis*
Chernobyl Hopper
Elk Hair Caddis
Goddard Caddis
Gold-Ribbed Hare's Ear
Gulper Special
Parachute Adams
Parachute Ant
Pheasant Tail Twist Nymph
Quigley Cripple
Renegade
Royal Wulff
Sadie Thompson Woolly Bugger
Serendipity
Sheep Creek Special
Stayner's Ducktail
Swannundaze Chironomid
TLF Midge
Turck's Tarantula

LOWLAND LAKES AND RESERVOIRS

I am not the most avid lake angler in Idaho—not by a long shot. However, I can't imagine a better way to spend a spring day—when the rivers and streams are blown out—than fishing a still water for bass or trout.

One of the most appealing aspects of lakes and reservoirs is the size of the fish you might catch. Still waters support large populations of aquatic insects, as well as baitfishes such as yellow perch, suckers, and shiners. Due to that abundance of forage, still-water trout grow much faster than their stream-born relatives, which must constantly fight the current to access food. In Idaho, it's not uncommon to land a 4- or 5-pound trout in a still water, and 10-pound-plus specimens exist in several waters throughout the state.

Typically, lake and reservoir fishing begins in earnest just as the ice departs in March, April, or, after an extremely persistent winter, May. At that time, trout concentrate on large food items, such as sculpins and other forage fishes. They also feed heavily on chironomids or midges.

As the water warms, aquatic insects emerge, and they are an important part of the trout's diet. Important early-season hatches include *Callibaetis* and *Baetis* mayflies, followed by caddisflies, damselflies and Pale Morning Duns.

Often, still-water trout fishing slows around mid-summer, but those fish may still be taken early or late in the day when water temperatures are cool. At that time, streamer patterns and terrestrials are your best choices.

When fall arrives and water temperatures cool, anglers again find *Callibaetis*, *Baetis* and chironomids on the water, along with grasshoppers, ants, beetles, and October caddis.

For warmwater species such as bass and bluegill, spring and fall offer the best opportunities, although mid-summer provides action in the morning and evening hours, extending into the dead of night.

Idaho's largemouth and smallmouth bass are particularly fond of streamers and topwater offerings such as mice and frogs. However, they will key on insects and I've taken them on size-16 Pale Morning Dun cripples at Carey Lake.

Northern pike are also available in northern Idaho, and they are most active during the spring and fall, when streamers and topwater offerings such as mice draw incredible strikes.

The following is a list of Idaho's top lowland lake and reservoir fisheries, plus a selection of flies that work best on those waters.

Brownlee Reservoir: A major impoundment of the Snake River, Brownlee is loaded with smallmouth bass and crappie. If you hit this reservoir on the right day, you may land and release a couple of dozen smallmouths.

Carey Lake: Located just east of Carey, this small water offers some 14-inch largemouth bass, plus some hand-sized bluegill. An excellent spring fishery, this lake is unproductive during summer, so carefully pick your time to visit.

Chesterfield Reservoir: Located just outside Chesterfield, Idaho, this reservoir kicks out some healthy rainbow trout during spring, early summer, and fall. Five-pound fish can be had, but most fish range from 12 to 16 inches.

Condie Reservoir: Located north of Preston, Condie offers largemouth bass that can exceed 20 inches. This is an excellent springtime destination.

Daniel's Reservoir: Daniel's Reservoir, located near Malad, is a good place to take a shot at a trophy rainbow-cutthroat hybrid. The limit allows 2 fish over 20 inches, but most fly fishers release their catch. Best fished during spring and fall, Daniel's Reservoir commonly produces 3- to 5-pound trout.

Henry's Lake: Located just inside the Montana border near Macks Inn, Henry's Lake is Idaho's top still-water trout fishery: The lake gives up an obscene number of 3- to 10-pound rainbow-cutthroat hybrids each year, and it also offers brook trout to 5 pounds. Because this lake is surrounded by private property, it is best fished by boat or float tube.

Island Park Reservoir: Not as popular as its northern neighbor, Henry's Lake, Island Park Reservoir produces some enormous brown trout, as well as some sizable rainbows and cutthroats. This reservoir has a hit-or-miss reputation, so don't judge it by a single visit. For a half-day or full-day excursion away from the Henry's Fork River, Island Park is an excellent option.

Lake Coeur d'Alene: This large northern Idaho water holds a variety of fish, but the northern pike is most accessible to the fly rodder. During the spring and again in the fall, northerns move into the shallow bays to prowl the weed lines. At that time a large streamer or topwater pattern can prove deadly.

Mackay Reservoir: Located in the Lost River drainage north of Mackay and south of Challis, Mackay Reservoir gives up some gracious catches of rainbow trout. The entire reservoir gives up fish, but fly fishers concentrate their efforts at the northern end, where the Big Lost River flows in.

Magic Reservoir: Located south of Sun Valley and north of Shoshone, Magic offers fly fishers excellent opportunities for rainbow and brown trout before the stream opener. Some large browns can be had here, but the average fish is a 12- to 15-inch rainbow.

Palisades Reservoir: When the ice comes off this reservoir, float tubers do well in the isolated bays. Large browns and big cutthroats and rainbows are the reward for battling cold water and, often, windy conditions. When fishing large streamer patterns, a fly fisher also as a chance to hook a lake trout, which run to 30 pounds.

FLIES FOR LOWLAND LAKES AND RESERVOIRS

Trout

Carey Special

CDC Biot ComparaDun *Callibaetis*

Chernobyl Hopper

Elk Hair October Caddis

Extended-Body Dun

Gulper Special

Lawson's Foam Beetle

Mackay Special

Magic Perch

Parachute Adams

Parachute Ant

Philo Betto

Quigley Cripple

Sadie Thompson Woolly Bugger

Sculpin Minnow

Serendipity

Sheep Creek Special

Slow Water Caddis

Sparkle Dun

Stayner's Ducktail

Swannundaze Chironomid

TLF Midge

Bass

Whitlock's Mouserat

Zonker

Pike

Dahlberg Diver

Mickey Finn

Northern Pike Fly

Whitlock's Mouserat, Black

FREESTONE STREAMS AND CREEKS

Freestone streams and creeks offer some of Idaho's best fly-fishing opportunities. However, they are vulnerable to the nuances of nature, especially snowmelt and runoff, so you should time your visit to these waters carefully.

Fortunately, Idaho abounds with freestone streams, so it's rarely difficult to find one that's fishing well. A particular stream might be blown out by spring runoff, but another may be in perfect shape and fishing nicely.

Many of Idaho's freestones close during the winter (November 30 through May), with several notable exceptions, including the Big Wood and Little Wood Rivers.

Although they offer attractive features, freestones also provide some of fly fishing's most challenging situations. For example, wading freestone streams is troublesome, if not downright terrifying in some cases, due to slippery rocks and fast flows (you should always wear a wading belt). At any given time, several hatches may be occurring simultaneously, which forces you to discern which insect the trout are feeding on, and to then choose a fly that matches the particular stage of the hatch (nymph, emerger, dun, spinner). Once you've made the proper selection, you must place your fly in the trout's path, and often without drag—not any easy task when fishing across varying currents. But as any savvy fly fisher will tell you, that is the appeal of freestone trout streams: They are extremely challenging on some occasions, and graciously generous on others.

Freestones typically fish well after spring runoff (and prior to runoff on streams that remain open throughout the winter). The fishing remains excellent through late spring, summer, and fall, when they offer many insect hatches.

On the typical freestone, you may find Green, Gray, and Brown Drake mayflies, Pale Morning Dun mayflies, Trico mayflies, Mahogany Dun mayflies, Pink Albert mayflies, and

Baetis mayflies. You'll see numerous caddis species, as well as stoneflies, including giant goldens, salmon flies (*Pteronarcys californica*), and little golden stoneflies. During late fall and winter, profuse midge hatches may bring fish to the top.

Although there are usually a number of insects to match on the surface, freestones also offer good subsurface angling, which usually produce a river's largest fish. Beadhead nymphs, crustacean patterns, and streamers are very effective on freestones, especially in the slack, deep-water pockets, where large trout prefer to hold.

No matter what freestone you choose to fish, arrive with an arsenal of flies. Situations change quickly on freestones, and that will influence your fly selection.

Below is a list of Idaho's top freestone streams and creeks, along with a selection of flies that work best on those waters.

Kelly Creek: One of Idaho's most beautiful waters, Kelly Creek is the consummate cutthroat trout stream. Far from any town, Kelly Creek still sees its share of pressure, so innovative fly patterns work well here. Kelly Creek's cutthroat average 12 to 16 inches, with a few reaching that magical 20-inch mark.

Lochsa River: Located just southwest of Missoula, Montana, the Lochsa is paralleled by a highway throughout its length. However, many places require the angler to trek down long, steep banks to gain access. That keeps many areas out of reach of the common angler. The Lochsa's rainbows and cutthroat trout are aggressive.

Middle Fork Salmon River: One of the wildest, remote sections of water in Idaho, the Middle Fork carves through the Frank Church River of No Return Wilderness. Rafting trips keep the river busy during the summer. However, during the fall, the Middle Fork is fairly well deserted. Whether you visit during the summer (after runoff) or the fall, you'll be treated to some of the best native west-slope cutthroat trout fishing in the world. These cutts average 8 to 15 inches, but 18-inchers aren't uncommon. For those who seek adventure with their fishing, this is an excellent option.

North Fork Clearwater River: There is an interesting phenomenon that occurs late each summer and early fall when large cutthroats depart Kelly Creek and teem into the North Fork Clearwater. At that time—usually from September 15th on—there are more large cutts in the Clearwater than in Kelly Creek. During the rest of the year, the North Fork's resident fish keep fly fishers busy as they devour a variety of attractor dry flies.

St. Joe River: Not nearly as prestigious as nearby Kelly Creek, the St. Joe offers remarkably good action for rainbow trout and cutthroats.

Selway River: If you are looking for solitude, the Selway is the place to be. One road leads into its headwaters and one tracks its lower end, but between those points the Selway flows through wilderness. To float the river (for experts only) you must obtain a limited-entry permit from the Forest Service. However, backpacking fly fishers and anglers on horseback can fish the river at their leisure. The river's cutthroats and occasional bull trout are not too fussy. General attractors work well here.

Upper Big Wood River: The Big Wood, which runs through Ketchum, Hailey, and Bellevue, is an excellent rainbow fishery. It also produces some nice browns during the fall, when the fish move out of Magic Reservoir and push through portions of the upper river. This stream offers excellent hatches, including Pale Morning Duns, Green Drakes, Tricos, *Baetis*, Mahogany Duns, Western Red Quills, and midges. The average rainbow runs 12 to 15 inches; however, larger fish can be had. If you hit this stream when the Green Drakes are in full swing, you'll never forget it.

FLIES FOR IDAHO'S FREESTONE RIVERS AND CREEKS

Bitch Creek Nymph

Box Canyon Stone

CDC Biot ComparaDun Trico

CDC Rusty Spinner

Chernobyl Hopper

Diving Caddis

Electric Caddis

Elk Hair Caddis

Elk Hair October Caddis

Emergent Sparkle Pupa

Goddard Caddis

Gold-Ribbed Hare's Ear

Hair-Wing Dun

Halfback Emerger

Improved Sofa Pillow

Kaufmann's Rubber Leg Stone, Black

Lawson's Green Drake Paradrake

Light Variant

Marcella's Trout Fly

Moose Mane Extended-Body Green Drake

October Caddis Larva

Parachute Adams

Parachute Ant

Pheasant Tail Twist Nymph

Philo Betto

Prince Nymph

Quigley Cripple

Sculpin Minnow

Sparkle Dun

Stimulator

Super Renegade

Turck's Tarantula

X-Caddis

Spring Creeks

There arrives a time in the lives of all passionate fly fishers when they can look in the mirror and safely say, "I've caught a hell of a lot of fish on the fly."

When that happens, their mindset often changes from being satisfied with small trout to desiring something larger. Some people might say that's just so they can pound their chests and brag about the giant fish they catch. But in my mind, searching for large fish encompasses something deeper—although I must admit, when I land a big one all my friends know about it.

Trying to catch large trout is one of the most challenging fly-fishing propositions, and that difficulty only increases when an angler chooses to fish a spring creek.

For fly fishers who judge the day by the number of trout brought to net, a spring creek is the last place they'd want to plant their boots. Spring creeks offer lessons in acute frustration.

However, some of us regard that challenge as the true beauty of a spring creek. We've caught enough small fish on easy waters, and left that spinning rod at home enough times, to quell our desire for recognition as a "fly fisher." We've decided that numbers of trout are not as important as challenge or quality. We rest assured that if we wanted to, we could run to our favorite ranch pond and bust sixty fish in a day. But that is not where our progression as fly fishers should end. That is not where challenge and reward rest. Instead, we should welcome new challenges, find merit in continually learning more about the ways of trout.

Once fly fishers reach that level, they must take stock of their actions, realize how far they have come and decide how deep they want to go. If they decide to wade deeper, at some point they'll end up at a spring creek. The fish are there, but the odds are poor. However, on any given cast they might

hook and hold a true leviathan, and on a dry fly no less—a
fish to release back into the creek and call it a day. After all,
why try to repeat perfection?

A day on a spring creek can solve many of life's myster-
ies. It can dissolve stress, heal broken hearts and dreams,
and make the frustrations of everyday life just a little more
bearable.

Perhaps that's the true beauty of a trout stream. You can
arrive with a dizzying array of complexities hanging over
your head like a nasty August thunderhead, and a while later
walk away with wet waders and a new outlook on life:
Catching big trout is everything, man!

If you're ready to accept extreme challenge and pit your
skills against some of the wariest trout in the world, then
you're ready to hit one of Idaho's premiere spring creeks.
Fortunately, Idaho offers two of the world's finest.

The following is a description of those creeks, plus a
selection of flies that work best on them.

Henry's Fork of the Snake River: Located in eastern
Idaho near Island Park, the Henry's Fork is one of the
world's most famous waters, and it attracts anglers from
many countries. And for good reason: The Henry's Fork
offers varied sections, lots of aquatic insects, and enormous
trout. However, that does not mean those fish are easy.

The Henry's Fork resembles a spring creek through a
section called Railroad Ranch, also referred to as Harriman
State Park.

Through summer and fall, the "Ranch" hosts healthy
emergences of Pale Morning Duns, March Brown Drakes
(*Rhithrogena*), *Ephemerella flavilinea*, Brown Drakes
(*Ephemera simulans*), Green Drakes, Gray Drakes, Tricos,
Baetis, and Mahogany Dun mayflies. Flying ants, grasshop-
pers, and beetles also show up in July, August, and
September. Craneflies, several caddis species including the
October caddis, and damselflies also draw fish to the surface.

With that much food at their disposal, Henry's Fork trout become incredibly selective, which means they inspect artificial flies closely before taking them. Many of the West's most technical patterns originated on the Henry's Fork, and in order to catch fish here, you must put them to use.

Silver Creek: Many anglers regard the Railroad Ranch section of the Henry's Fork River as the most difficult water in Idaho, if not the entire West. However, I consider Silver Creek, with its healthy population of rainbow and brown trout, as the ultimate angling challenge.

Silver Creek winds through Camas Prairie, which is south of Sun Valley, and it offers a plethora of insect hatches, not to mention some excellent terrestrial action.

Through summer and fall, anglers must be prepared to match Brown Drake, Pale Morning Dun, *Baetis*, Trico, and Mahogany Dun mayflies. Grasshoppers, ants, and beetles are also on the water during late summer and early fall. Craneflies and damselflies are also present, and imitations of those big bugs sometimes draw strikes when all else fails.

Because of Silver Creek's aquatic and terrestrial smorgasbord, your fly box should be loaded with patterns that represent all of those insects at their various life stages. When all else fails, a weighted nymph or large streamer may produce, so it pays to carry a number of subsurface flies as well.

Flies for Idaho's Spring Creeks
> Brassie
> CDC Biot ComparaDun *Callibaetis*
> CDC Biot ComparaDun Trico
> CDC Rusty Spinner
> Elk Hair Caddis
> Emergent Sparkle Pupa
> Hair-Wing Dun
> Halfback Emerger
> Hare's Ear Rubber Leg Nymph

Hatch Master

Hemingway Caddis

Henry's Fork Hopper

Lawson's Brown Drake Nymph

Lawson's Foam Beetle

Lawson's Green Drake Paradrake

Loop-Wing Dun

No-Hackle

North Fork Fly

Parachute Adams

Parachute Ant

Pheasant Tail Twist Nymph

Prince Nymph

Quigley Cripple

Sadie Thompson Woolly Bugger

Sculpin Minnow

Sparkle Dun

Spent Partridge Caddis

Tailwaters

Because of their fertile, controlled flows, tailwaters provide some of Idaho's best fishing for large trout. Steelhead and smallmouth bass also call Idaho's tailwaters home, but opportunities for those species are limited.

Tailwaters, which are streams regulated by a dam, offer excellent insect hatches, so it will benefit you to have a variety of flies. For example, on the South Fork Snake, which possibly is Idaho's best tailwater, you may encounter a variety of insects on the water simultaneously. On any given day in July, you may find Pale Morning Duns, *Baetis*, caddisflies, salmon flies, and Yellow Sallies. You may also find ants and beetles.

Because tailwaters provide a plethora of food, trout can be as selective as they like. Therefore, fly patterns must specifically imitate various stages of insect emergences. For example, if a trout is feeding selectively on stillborn and emergent Pale Morning Duns, you're not going to hook it on an attractor such as a Royal Wulff or a Renegade. Instead, a Sparkle Dun or a Quigley Cripple, which offer a trailing shuck as does the natural, are your best bets.

Tailwaters may demand much from an angler. However, they make up for their quirky temperament by offering thousands of mature trout per mile. And this, as you'll find, is an equitable trade-off.

Below is a list of Idaho's top tailwaters, along with a good selection of flies.

Big Lost River: Once the semiprivate playground of Mackay and Sun Valley anglers, the Big Lost is now fished by anglers from all over the state. The Big Lost offers sizable rainbow trout that eagerly take nymphs, streamers, and the occasional dry fly.

The Big Lost runs high and fast during the early season, and its brushy banks force anglers to wade, so it's best to avoid it then. By July the water has dropped, and you can negotiate the river then with studded wading boots and a good measure of courage. The best area for large fish twists through the willows and cottonwoods just north of Mackay. For a different scene, try the East Fork of the Big Lost, a freestone section that flows through Copper Basin.

Henry's Fork River: The tailwater section of the Henry's Fork begins at Island Park Dam and extends to the Railroad Ranch at Island Park.

Throughout that stretch, which is commonly called Box Canyon, anglers ply the water for large rainbow trout. Prime fishing can be had in the early season when *Baetis* mayflies are accompanied by hoards of salmon flies. Those big bugs bring trout to the top, but during the rest of the season Box Canyon is best fished with nymphs.

South Fork Boise River: Located just an hour southwest of Boise, the South Fork Boise hosts excellent insect hatches—*Baetis,* Pale Morning Duns, Pink Alberts, salmon flies, golden stoneflies, Yellow Sallies—and holds good numbers of large rainbow trout. The river is best floated during the early season. After mid-July the flows settle down and anglers can find prime wade-fishing.

South Fork Snake River: The South Fork Snake is regarded as one of the top cutthroat fisheries in the world. As a bonus, this eastern Idaho water offers rainbow trout and some giant browns. Due to huge releases from Palisades Dam, the South Fork runs high and roily through mid-July. Prime fishing generally begins in late July and extends through October.

FLIES FOR IDAHO'S TAILWATERS

> Box Canyon Stone
> CDC Biot ComparaDun Trico
> CDC Rusty Spinner
> Diving Caddis

Electric Caddis
Elk Hair Caddis
Elk Hair October Caddis
Emergent Sparkle Pupa
Goddard Caddis
Hair-Wing Dun
Hare's Ear Nymph
Henry's Fork Golden Stone
Henry's Fork Hopper
Improved Sofa Pillow
J.J. Special
Kaufmann's Rubber Leg Stone
Light Variant
Master Nymph (Epoxy)
No-Hackle
October Caddis Larva
Parachute Adams
Pheasant Tail Twist Nymph
Prince Nymph
Quigley Cripple
Sculpin Minnow
Serendipity
Sparkle Dun
Stimulator
Swannundaze Chironomid
Turck's Tarantula
X-Caddis

CHAPTER FOUR
Best Flies for Idaho's Gamefishes

RAINBOW TROUT

POSSIBLY IDAHO'S MOST POPULAR GAMEFISH, rainbow trout are found throughout the state in a variety of water types. Whether you fish a lake, reservoir, river, stream, or spring creek, you are likely to catch a rainbow.

Rainbows are the fly fisher's darling for two reasons: They eat dry flies like candy, and they are terrific fighters with a propensity to jump.

Good patterns for rainbow trout cover the big-name hatches, such as Pale Morning Duns, *Baetis,* Tricos; Green, Gray, and Brown Drakes; Mahogany Duns, and *Callibaetis* mayflies. Standard caddis species, such as *Brachycentrus, Hydropsyche,* and *Cheumatopsyche,* can be matched with numerous patterns. Big stoneflies get a rainbow trout's attention, especially in late spring and early summer, and there are a number of patterns that accurately imitate the adult stage of those large insects.

Although rainbows are most often taken on surface flies, they also feed heavily on nymphs, and the standard "Big Three"—the Pheasant Tail Nymph, the Hare's Ear Nymph, and the Prince Nymph—produce well. During winter and spring, rainbows (especially large specimens) turn their attention to forage fishes. Streamer patterns such as Woolly Buggers, Zonkers, Rabbit Strip Leeches, and Mickey Finns all draw strikes. And during late summer and fall, you would not want to approach a rainbow trout river without a few hopper and ant patterns in your fly box.

In lakes and reservoirs rainbows take streamer patterns eagerly, especially near shore in spring and fall. The best insect hatch on still waters occur in late May, June, and July, when the damselflies come off. During that time, a variety of damsel patterns draw strikes, and I am not aware of a better time to take a large rainbow trout.

From winter through summer, chironomids, which are also called midges, are extremely effective on still waters, and there literally are hundreds of imitations to match the diminutive two-winged fly.

Listed below are some of the best patterns for rainbow trout—flies you should carry in you vest at all times.

Mayflies
>   CDC Rusty Spinner
>   Gulper Special
>   Hare's Ear Nymph
>   Parachute Adams
>   Pheasant Tail Twist Nymph
>   Quigley Cripple
>   Sparkle Dun

Caddisflies
>   Elk Hair Caddis
>   Emergent Sparkle Pupa
>   Goddard Caddis
>   Prince Nymph
>   Slow Water Caddis
>   Spent Partridge Caddis
>   Stimulator

Stoneflies
>   Improved Sofa Pillow
>   Turck's Tarantula

Terrestrials
>   Bing's Hopper
>   Parachute Ant

Damselflies
>   Marabou Damsel
>   Marv's Fly

Streamers
>   Canadian Brown Mohair Leech

Stayner's Ducktail
Woolly Bugger, Brown, Black, Olive
Zonker, White

CUTTHROAT TROUT

NAMED FOR THE TWO ORANGE SLASHES it exhibits on the underside of its lower jaw, the cutthroat trout is an Idaho original, a beautiful native fish that puts smiles on anglers' faces.

In terms of aggressive feeding behavior, the cutthroat cannot be beat, making them one of the easiest gamefish to catch in Idaho. And that's why they're such a treat to fish for—especially after you've been tested by demanding rainbow and brown trout on difficult waters. Because of their eagerness to take—they have a particular fondness for large, bushy dry flies—the cutthroat is a wonderful fish for beginning or young fly anglers.

Cutthroats generally respond to a variety of dry-fly attractors, including as the Royal Wulff, the Trude, the Parachute Adams, and the Renegade. They'll also take an array of suggestive nymph patterns, such as the Hare's Ear, the Pheasant Tail, and the Prince Nymph. Only occasionally are specific imitations required to match a particular stage of the hatch, such as on Idaho's heavily fished Kelly Creek.

Northern Idaho's streams—including Kelly Creek and the Lochsa, the Clearwater, and the Selway Rivers—are accurately described as the last bastion for native westslope cutthroats. Cutthroat trout inhabit the lowland rivers of eastern Idaho, such as the South Fork Snake and the Teton, and they're found in many high-mountain lakes as well.

Yes, the cutthroat trout is foolish fish, easily enticed by artificial flies. But they are also an Idaho native—one that was here before all the imports—and they deserve a good measure of respect.

Listed below are some of the best patterns for cutthroat trout.

Attractors
  Royal Wulff
  St. Joe Special
  Trude
  Turck's Tarantula

Mayflies
  CDC Rusty Spinner
  Hair Wing Dun
  Hare's Ear Nymph
  Moose Mane Extended-Body Green Drake
  Parachute Adams
  Pheasant Tail Twist Nymph
  Quigley Cripple

Caddisflies
  Elk Hair Caddis
  Elk Hair October Caddis
  Emergent Sparkle Pupa
  Goddard Caddis
  October Caddis Larva, Beadhead
  Prince Nymph
  Stimulator

Stoneflies
  Henry's Fork Golden Stonefly
  Henry's Fork Salmon Fly
  Improved Sofa Pillow
  Turck's Tarantula

Terrestrials
  Bing's Hopper
  Parachute Ant

Streamers
  Canadian Brown Mohair Leech
  Stayner's Ducktail
  Woolly Bugger, Brown, Black, Olive
  Zonker White

BROWN TROUT

Imported from Europe, the brown trout gained a foothold in Idaho's waters during this century, providing an opportunity that most fly fishers relish. Brown trout are considered the most wary of Idaho's trout species, and their temperamental nature provides serious challenges for the angler. However, they attain large size, and they're a perfectly beautiful fish to look at, their yellow hue accentuated with black-lined, flaming-red spots.

Brown trout are found throughout Idaho in all water types, with the exception of high-mountain lakes. In reservoirs, browns can grow to enormous size.

To fool brown trout that are keyed in on insect hatches, anglers are required to use specific imitations. Gaudy streamers will attract the attention of opportunistic fish, and are a good bet to take a large brown. In fact, when a brown trout reaches the 20-inch mark, which is quite common in Idaho, its dietary preference switches from aquatic insects to larger food forms such as frogs, mice, minnows, and even small ducks. (Brown trout exceeding 20 pounds have been taken from Idaho's rivers, so they are capable of swallowing a duck.)

Large brown trout will rise to the surface when the opportunity warrants it. If you're looking to take a big brown on a dry fly, there are specific occasions that increase your odds. Try fishing the Brown Drake hatches on Silver Creek and the Henry's Fork, as well as the giant stonefly hatches on the South Fork Snake and the Henry's Fork. During the heat of late July, August, and September, hopper patterns are a good bet to take large browns.

By late September, most of Idaho's brown trout are preparing to spawn, and that instinct brings the largest fish—trout that sat under the cutbanks all summer—out into the open. For the serious streamer angler, there is no better time to try for a giant brown.

Below are listed some of the best patterns for brown trout.

Attractors

Royal Wulff

Trude

Turck's Tarantula

Mayflies

CDC Rusty Spinner

Hair-Wing Dun

Hare's Ear Nymph

Lawson's Brown Drake Nymph

Moose Mane Extended-Body Green Drake

Parachute Adams

Pheasant Tail Twist Nymph

Quigley Cripple

Sparkle Dun

Caddisflies

Elk Hair Caddis

Elk Hair October Caddis

Emergent Sparkle Pupa

Goddard Caddis

October Caddis Larva, Beadhead

Prince Nymph

Slow Water Caddis

Stimulator

Stoneflies

Henry's Fork Golden Stonefly

Henry's Fork Salmon Fly

Improved Sofa Pillow

Turck's Tarantula

Terrestrials

Bing's Hopper

Chernobyl Hopper

Parachute Ant

Streamers

Canadian Brown Mohair Leech

Master Nymph (Epoxy)

Sculpin Minnow

Stayner's Ducktail

Woolly Bugger, Brown, Black, Olive

Zonker, White

BROOK TROUT

BROOK TROUT DO NOT RANK HIGH on the Idaho fly fisher's list, yet they do provide excellent angling opportunities, with some specimens attaining large size.

Possibly Idaho's best-known population of brook trout exists in Henry's Lake, where most fish range from 1 to 3 pounds, but where it is possible to hook a 5-pounder.

Elsewhere in the state, brook trout do not attain such impressive sizes, but they do have attributes. Where Idaho's brook trout are typically found, in small freestone streams and beaver ponds, they exist in large numbers and are extremely competitive, making them easy to catch on a variety of flies. Idaho's brook trout waters serve as a great learning ground for beginning and young fly fishers.

The following is a list of some of the best flies for Idaho's brook trout.

Attractors

Royal Wulff

Trude

Turck's Tarantula

Mayflies

Hare's Ear Nymph

Parachute Adams

Pheasant Tail Twist Nymph

Quigley Cripple

Sparkle Dun

Caddisflies

Elk Hair Caddis

Goddard Caddis

Prince Nymph

Stimulator

Stoneflies

Turck's Tarantula

Damselflies

Marabou Damsel

Terrestrials

Bing's Hopper

Parachute Ant

Streamers

Canadian Brown Mohair Leech

Halloween Leech (particularly for Henry's Lake)

Stayner's Ducktail

Woolly Bugger, Brown, Black, Olive

WHITEFISH

NOT HIGHLY REGARDED BY FLY FISHERS, the commonly caught whitefish is often chucked into the brush to rot. And that's a shame. Whitefish are not my favorite fish, but each one deserves a measure of respect: They are native to Idaho's waters and they are a living creature. Whenever I catch one, I quickly remove the hook and gently release my catch.

Whitefish are found in great numbers in almost every stream in the state. They average 6 to 12 inches, but 17- to 20-inch specimens are possible. Large whitefish put a good bend in a 4- or 5-weight fly rod, and more than once I've been fooled into thinking that the whitefish at the end of my line was actually a large trout.

Whitefish often hold in large schools near the bottom of a stream. So once you locate them, you can often take fish after fish. Whitefish are especially fond of flashy nymphs, but they will take a variety of flies. So no matter where you encounter them, you're likely to have something in your fly box that will do the trick. When conditions warrant it, such as the Brown Drake hatch on the Henry's Fork, whitefish will take dry flies.

Although anglers generally bemoan their presence, I've

seen whitefish save the day when trout were hard to come by. The following are some of the best flies for Idaho's whitefish.

Mayflies

CDC Rusty Spinner

Flashback Hare's Ear Nymph

Flashback Pheasant Tail Nymph, beadhead

Light Cahill

Parachute Adams

Sparkle Dun

Caddisflies

Cased Caddis Larva

Elk Hair Caddis

Emergent Sparkle Pupa

Neon Prince Nymph

Stoneflies

Kaufmann's Rubber Leg Stone, Black

Mormon Girl

Streamers

Woolly Bugger, Brown

STEELHEAD

ONE OF IDAHO'S MOST AMAZING FISH is the steelhead, an anadromous rainbow trout that swims over 500 miles from the Pacific Ocean to reach its natal waters to spawn. (And you thought you had it bad!)

In Idaho, steelhead are not the bright-chrome demons you may find in the coastal streams of Washington and Oregon. In fact, by the time they reach Idaho, most steelhead are slashed with crimson and gold, and they weigh much less than they did when they left the sea. Cartwheeling acrobats they are not. However, any gamefish of 25 to 30 inches that harbors such a will to reproduce is a fish to be appreciated.

In Idaho, steelhead may be found on the Salmon, the Little Salmon, the Snake, and the Clearwater Rivers. However, dams on the Snake River contribute heavily to the decline of steelhead: Their current range is only a sliver of their native ground. If you live in Idaho and are old enough to vote, help those steelhead and support the removal of the Snake River dams. Idaho's steelhead depend on us.

Idaho's steelhead are not tremendously difficult to catch; however, angling tactics differ from those commonly used on Idaho's other salmonids. The basic difference in presentation is called the "steelhead swing." Most often steelhead prefer a swinging fly, one that slices sideways through the water, presenting a full broadside profile. And often, steelhead prefer the fly low in the water column. For that reason, sink-tip lines are extremely important to steelhead anglers. However, a floating line works in a pinch, especially when fishing a dry fly.

Typically, Idaho's steelhead fly fishers go with sparsely dressed patterns when the water is low and clear. During the spring, or when rains have clouded the waters, larger, heavily dressed flies prove more effective. The following is a list of some of the best patterns for Idaho steelhead.

Steelhead Flies

> Black Bunny Leech
> Boss
> Fall Favorite
> Fifi
> Freight Train
> Green Butt Skunk
> Muddler Minnow
> N. A. Steelhead Bugger (aka Volcano Bugger)
> October Caddis Larva

BASS

BASS TAKE A BACK SEAT TO IDAHO'S SALMONID species, and that isn't exactly fair. Largemouth bass are spread throughout Idaho, and offer excellent angling opportunities extending from the panhandle all the way to the southern deserts just north of the Utah and Nevada state lines.

Although largemouth bass can be taken beneath the surface on a variety of nymphs and streamers, most fly fishers pursue them on the surface, where bass really come into their own: They attack surface patterns with vengeance.

Bass are not overly picky when choosing their meal, so almost any surface pattern, from a size-16 Parachute Adams to a giant mouse imitation, could draw strikes.

Typically, bass are most active in spring and fall, and during the early-morning and late-evening hours of summer. The dead of night is an especially good time to fish for light-shy lunker bass. Of course, night-fishing presents its own set of quandaries, such as giant rattlesnakes swimming around your float tube, so only hard-cores need apply.

Decent opportunities exist for smallmouth bass in the Snake River impoundments, including Brownlee and Oxbow Reservoirs. Smallmouth, too, are aggressive fish, and subsurface patterns bring hearty strikes. Once located, schools of smallmouths can provide fast action for fly fishers who use streamer patterns with sink-tip or full-sinking lines. Listed here are some of the best flies for Idaho's bass.

Subsurface Flies
>   Blond Stayner
>   Canadian Brown Mohair Leech
>   Clouser's Crayfish
>   Mickey Finn
>   Muddler Minnow
>   Rabbit-Strip Leech
>   Woolly Buggers, Olive, Black, and Brown

Surface Flies
>   Muddler Minnow
>   Whitlock's Mouserat

NORTHERN PIKE

Nicknamed the "water wolf," northern pike are truly one of Idaho's fiercest predators. Streamlined and built for speed, the pike preys on small fish and mammals with amazing agility.

Northern pike inhabit many of north Idaho's lakes, including giant Lake Coeur d'Alene. Although northern pike in Idaho average 4 to 7 pounds, you could hook one exceeding 30 pounds on any given cast.

Typically pursued during spring and fall, when they inhabit shallow, weedy shorelines, northerns are somewhat overlooked by fly rodders. Most are taken by bait fishers, who toss minnows suspended beneath a cork. That's a shame, for there may not be a more exciting moment in a fly fisher's life than when a big northern streaks across the surface to slash at a large streamer.

Northern pike are not too picky about what they eat, but they do seem cognizant of color; they may pound a black streamer one day, and nothing but red or yellow the next. For that reason, it pays to experiment.

Idaho's pike can be taken on a variety of flies, but one characteristic remains constant: They want a pattern that is worth their effort—and that means big.

Bass poppers made of deer hair and cork are very effective for shallow-water pike. Double Bunny Leeches and large saltwater patterns such as Lefty's Deceiver produce strikes as well. Because pike often inhabit weedy areas, it makes sense to tie your flies with weedguards. Northern pike have wicked teeth, so steel leaders will prevent them from breaking off.

More Resources

On Idaho and Environs

Jacklin, Bob, and Gary LaFontaine. *Fly Fishing the Yellowstone in the Park.* Audio Tape. Helena, Montana: Greycliff Publishing Company, 1988.

Joye, W. David. *Silver Creek Journal.* River Journal Series. Portland, Oregon: Frank Amato Publications, 1993.

Kustich, Rick. *Salmon River.* River Journal Series. Portland, Oregon: Frank Amato Publications, 1995.

Lawson, Mike, and Gary LaFontaine. *Fly Fishing the Henry's Fork.* Audio tape. Helena, Montana: Greycliff Publishing Company, 1987.

Mathews, Craig, and Clayton Molinero. *Yellowstone Fly-Fishing Guide.* New York: Lyons and Burford, 1997.

Osthoff, Rich. *Fly Fishing the Rocky Mountain Backcountry.* Mechanicsburg, Pennsylvania: Stackpole Books, 1998.

Parks, Richard. *Fishing Yellowstone National Park.* Helena, Montana: Falcon Press, 1998.

Retallic, Ken, and Rocky Barker. *Flyfisher's Guide to Idaho.* Gallatin Gateway, Montana: Wilderness Adventures Press, 1996.

Shorett, Dave. *Olympic Mountains Fishing Guide: Olympic National Park and Olympic Peninsula Lakes and Streams.* Seattle: LakeStream Publications, 1996.

Staples, Bruce. *Yellowstone Park.* River Journal Series. Portland, Oregon: Frank Amato Publications, 1996.

Thomas, Greg. *The Clark Fork River.* River Journal Series. Portland, Oregon: Frank Amato Publications, 1998.

Tullis, Larry. *Henry's Fork.* River Journal Series. Portland, Oregon: Frank Amato Publications, 1995.

On Flies and Fly Tying

Brooks, Charles E. *Fishing Yellowstone Waters.* New York: Lyons Books, 1984.

Hughes, Dave. *Trout Flies.* Mechanicsburg, Pennsylvania: Stackpole Books, 1999.

Hughes, Dave. *Western Streamside Guide.* Portland, Oregon: Frank Amato Publications, 1987.

Hughes, Dave. *Wet Flies: Tying and Fishing Soft-Hackle, Winged and Wingless Wets, and Fuzzy Nymphs*. Mechanicsburg, Pennsylvania: Stackpole Books, 1995.

Hughes, Dave, and Rick Hafeley. *The Complete Book of Western Hatches: An Angler's Entomology and Fly Pattern Field Guide*. Portland, Oregon: Frank Amato Publications, 1981.

Inland Empire Fly Fishing Club and Fenton Roskelley. *Flies of the Northwest*. River Journal Series. Portland, Oregon: Frank Amato Publications, 1998.

Kaufmann, Randall. *Tying Dry Flies: The Complete Dry Fly Instruction and Pattern Manual*. Portland, Oregon: Western Fisherman's Press, 1995.

Kaufmann, Randall. *Tying Nymphs: Tie Perfect Nymphs with Speed, Ease, and Efficiency*. Portland, Oregon: Western Fisherman's Press, 1994.

LaFontaine, Gary. *Trout Flies: Proven Patterns*. Helena, Montana: Greycliff Publishing Company, 1993.

Mathews, Craig, and John Juracek. *Fly Patterns of Yellowstone*. West Yellowstone, Montana: Blue Ribbon Flies, 1987.

Schollmeyer, Jim, and Ted Leeson. *Trout Flies of the West: Best Contemporary Patterns from the Rockies, West*. Portland, Oregon: Frank Amato Publications, 1998.

Staples, Bruce. *Snake River Country Flies and Waters*. Portland, Oregon: Frank Amato Publications, 1991.

On Bugs

Caucci, Al, and Bob Nastasi. *Hatches II*. New York: Lyons and Burford, 1986.

Juracek, John, and Craig Mathews. *Fishing Yellowstone Hatches*. West Yellowstone, Montana: Blue Ribbon Flies, 1992.

Knopp, Malcolm, and Robert Cormier. *Mayflies: An Angler's Study of Trout Water Ephemeroptera*. Helena, Montana: Greycliff Publishing Company, 1997.

LaFontaine, Gary. *Caddisflies*. New York: Lyons and Burford, 1981.

Schollmeyer, Jim. *Hatch Guide for Lakes: Naturals and Their Imitations for Stillwater Trout Fishing*. Portland, Oregon: Frank Amato Publications, 1995.

Schollmeyer, Jim. *Hatch Guide for Western Streams*. Portland, Oregon: Frank Amato Publications, 1997.

On Technique

Brooks, Charles E. *Nymph Fishing for Larger Trout.* New York: Lyons and Burford, 1983.

Cordes, Ron. *Flyfishing for Backpackers.* 2d Ed. Rigby, Idaho: Troutbeck, 1992.

Engerbretson, Dave. *Tight Lines, Bright Water.* Moscow, Idaho: Solstice Press, 1986.

Judy, John. *Slack Line Strategies for Fly Fishing.* Mechanicsburg, Pennsylvania: Stackpole Books, 1994.

LaFontaine, Gary. *The Dry Fly, New Angles.* Helena, Montana: Greycliff Publishing Company, 1990.

LaFontaine, Gary. *Fly Fishing the Mountain Lakes.* Helena, Montana: Greycliff Publishing Company, 1998.

Shewey, John. *Alpine Angler: A Fly Fisher's Guide to the Western Wilderness.* Portland, Oregon: Frank Amato Publications, 1995.

Smith, Robert H. *Native Trout of North America.* Portland, Oregon: Frank Amato Publications, 1994.

Streeks, Neal. *Drift Boat Strategies: Rowing and Fishing Skills for the Western Angler.* Boulder, Colorado: Pruett Press, 1997.

INDEX

Bolded numbers indicate main entries.